T0304412

INTERGENERATIONAL HARMONY

INTERGENERATIONAL HARMONY

Unleashing the Strategic Power of Generational Synergy

BY

ARPAN S. YAGNIK
The Pennsylvania State University, USA

United Kingdom – North America – Japan – India
Malaysia – China

Emerald Publishing Limited
Emerald Publishing, Floor 5, Northspring, 21-23 Wellington Street, Leeds LS1 4DL

First edition 2024

Reprints and permissions service
Contact: www.copyright.com

British Library Cataloguing in Publication Data
A catalogue record for this book is available from the British Library

ISBN: 978-1-83549-161-4 (Print)
ISBN: 978-1-83549-160-7 (Online)
ISBN: 978-1-83549-162-1 (Epub)

Printed and bound by CPI Group (UK) Ltd, Croydon, CR0 4YY

INVESTOR IN PEOPLE

I dedicate this book to Daya, Nick, Sebastian, Alena, John, and Imad. They provided the initial sunshine, water, and nutrients for the idea of Intergenerational Harmony to germinate.

I dedicate this to my nieces and nephews: Saumya, Shreya, Hetvi, Rutvi, Urja, Hridit, Nisarg, Pranshu, Sharanya, Amay, Aashriya, Aarohi, Hitaay, Surya, Kahan, and Aanya. They are the future generation of my family, Bharat, and Earth.

I dedicate this book to the young tribal children of Anand Niketan Eklavya Residential School in Kaprada, India, whose rejuvenating presence and unhinged laughter strengthened my faith in this work. They are the future of Bharat and Earth.

And finally, I dedicate this book to the generations that have arrived and gone and the generations that are yet to arrive to go.

CONTENTS

FOREWORD

This project is a comet in my life. It appeared out of nowhere and has illuminated my life for the past two and a half years. I hope that now as it moves out of my hands, it illuminates many more lives and generations. It started with the sensitization that every organization I was affiliated with was trying to include youngsters and everyone was struggling. Why was everyone struggling, I had no idea. But once I firmly knew that this was a problem, I decided that something needs to be done about this.

The first opportunity presented itself when I found myself working with a very small group of incredible individuals to plan a global gathering for Initiatives of Change. All the members of the global movement were invited to participate in it. I proposed Intergenerational Harmony as one of the three options for a theme that the event could be anchored around. Everyone gravitated somehow toward Intergenerational Harmony. The work began and many more came forward to lend their helping hand. The culmination of the work came in the form of a three-day event with a vast array of participants from all time zones. The thematic aim of the three days was to increase Intergenerational Harmony by reducing generational biases.

This three-day experiment in increasing Intergenerational Harmony was insightfully successful. I got a firsthand idea of what it is to organize such purposeful events and what level of positive and negative outcomes can be derived from it. I was enriched and energized, but most importantly, I realized that organizing events that focused on Intergenerational Harmony, even on a smaller scale, is tremendously important for organizations and enterprises of all sorts. The need for this was greater than I had imagined initially.

After this experience, as I grew more convinced with the need to bridge the gap between generations, I started thinking of ways to do so. But there did not exist a framework or a guidance tool to do so. Being an academic, I thought of one of the most obvious things to do. Think and write. And that's how the journey began. ERTH was conceptualized and is offered in this book to all those who want to organize small or big events in their family or religion or enterprise or classroom to enhance Intergenerational Harmony.

I now put this book in your hands with the hope that it illuminates aptly to help Intergenerational Harmony materialize and enhance around and in you.

ACKNOWLEDGMENTS

I acknowledge the patience of all those with whom I have shared the idea of transforming my idea into a book. I am forever grateful for the encouragement and guidance supplied by respected and revered Prof Sheth. His words were, "Arpan this is important. Get it out as soon as possible." I also acknowledge Madison who got this project onto a runway. I acknowledge the interest and enthusiasm that Daniel Ridge had in this project from the get-go. His confidence in the merit of the project meant a lot to me when I had little to go. I acknowledge the entire editorial team who has worked on this project. I acknowledge all the people in my life who do not belong to my generation for enriching me and my understanding about multigenerationality through your presence in my life.

1

MULTIGENERATIONALITY IS HERE TO STAY

As a species, humans are experiencing multigenerational existence for the first time. Five different generations of humans with distinct psychosocial and sociocultural characteristics are living and competing for resources and agency at the same time. Implicitly, every generation is contending for dominance. Each generation has its own competitive advantages and disadvantages over others. Disparities in the abilities and agency of different generations in addition to inadequately available guidance in navigating the multigenerational existence have steered humanity to the cusp of a dangerous generational conflict.

Generational conflicts that arise due to the mismanagement of Multigenerationality manifest in myriad of ways from global to local levels. I will discuss some selected instances of generational conflicts such as the generational opposition against the 54 nuclear plants in Japan, generational opposition in China against pollution, the story behind the National Sorry Day in Australia, generational opposition in exploiting mother nature in the United States, and more later in the book. The impacts of generational conflicts are seen broadly in five macrosectors. But more importantly I will also offer strategies to enhance ERTH.

Humanity and its institutions have not even fully emerged from the prevailing class conflict. The addition of generational conflict is bound to add more burden on the already overburdened ecosystem. The new generational conflict is giving birth to unimagined challenges and struggles that are burning bridges rapidly, which would have otherwise hastened humanity's march to progress. Inept interest and lack of intelligent insights about issues that arise in the era of multigenerational existence are unfavorable to human civilization's growth and wellbeing. All human enterprises and institutions are bleeding due to inability of handling multigenerational existence. In this chapter, let us understand Multigenerationality and some of the foundational ways to understand generations and its categories.

MULTIGENERATIONALITY

The concept of Multigenerationality is explained and defined based on the concept of Convergence.[1] Multigenerationality is defined as the coming together of multiple generations (demographic or mindset based) with distinctly unique generational identities in the 21st century society. Great grandfathers and great grandmothers, for a vast majority of humanity, have existed only in stories and conversations. With medical advances and improved lifestyles, being able to coexist with great grandparents is a reality for many today. Multigenerationality is a phenomenon where members of different generations are living on the same planet sharing the same natural resources at the same time.

Multigenerationality is a relatively new phenomenon where individuals are either working and/or living with other individuals that belong to two or more generations. To properly understand Multigenerationality, it is important to look at the two fundamental ways in which generations that make up Multigenerationality in the 21st century can be comprehended. There are two types of Multigenerationality.

DEMOGRAPHIC OR AGE BASED

When demographically broken down, the populations living now can be broadly categorized into five generations. These generations are determined based on their respective years of birth. The Pew Research Center and Purdue University[2] provide excellent guidance and insight into these five generations. The five generations are labeled as The Silent Generation, Baby Boomers, Generation X, Millennials, and Generation Z. In demographic multigenerational convergence members of two or more generations come together in one household or working space. For example, when in a household family members form Generation X, Millennials, and Generation Z are living together. Each of the generational category will be elaborated in detail below.

THE SILENT GENERATION

Individuals that are born between 1925–1945 qualify to be a part of the Silent Generation. They are also referred to as the traditionalists. Members of this generation, like all the other generations, have a distinct personal and cultural identity. The great depression and the World War II were the two major events that occurred during the formative years of this generation. Both these catastrophic events have left a deep imprint on the Silent Generation's motivations, communication style, and worldview. Members of the Silent Generation are typically considered as loyal, dependable, and straightforward.

Members of the Silent Generation are farthest removed from some of the more recent forms of technological advances. They are the generation that would still send an annual newsletter through postal mail giving a sneak peek into their life and activities over the past year. They are naturally inclined to utilize means of communication that have a personal touch as opposed to some perceivably impersonal and group formats of communicating. They are typically of the worldview where age is a sign of seniority. They don't mind individualism but are much more amenable to obedience and collective thinking. They still observe and hold reverence for hierarchy and believe in working hard to advance in the hierarchical structures.

World War II was the most influential historic event in the lives of the Silent Generation. The Great Depression shaped the ethics and code of conduct and much of the world view for this generation making them big believers of saving as a core life ethic. Savings are important for this generation. Saving for a rainy day is something this generation has tried hard to impart to the members of other generations. Indulging in excess and vagary in spending is looked down upon by this generation. Frugality and fiscal conservatism are preferred because of what they experienced and learned from. Both frugality and fiscal conservatism are considered as a successful strategy to survive the uncertain and unknown tomorrow. Decisions of today are made giving prominence to tomorrow and the day after by this generation.

BABY BOOMERS

The population born from 1946 to 1964 is categorized as the Baby Boomers. They occupy the highest number of seats in the US House and the US Senate at the moment, playing a key role, in devising policies and the meta structure for code of conduct and ethics for Americans to abide and live by.[3] Although Baby

Boomers are consistently exiting the workforce, according to an estimate 10,000/day, 65% of the respondents from a sample of Baby Boomers expressed their desire to continue to be a part of the workforce past the age of 65.[4] And in 2018, 29% Boomers were still a part of the workforce and/or were actively applying for jobs.

Major events that shaped the motivations and worldview of this generation are the Civil Rights Movement, Vietnam War, Cold War, Cuban Missile Crisis, Man on Moon, JFK assassination, and the Watergate Scandal. Baby Boomers are also contributing substantially to the growing rate of gray divorces among the 50 years or older American population, where the rates of divorce have doubled from what they were in 1990.[5] They believe that success cannot be easily achieved without making sacrifices. And one needs to pay her or his or their dues for achieving success and popularity. Baby boomers are good team players and are in general optimistic and competitive individuals.

GENERATION X

The Generation X population, which is popularly known as Gen X, is the group of people that were born between 1965 and 1980. This generation currently makes up a majority of start-up founders. Some of the major events that have shaped this generation are the dot-com boom, the fall of Berlin Wall, and the HIV-AIDS epidemic. This is the generation, which started thinking more about their own personal and professional interests as far as workplace growth is concerned over the company's interest. Generation X individuals favor diversity along with work–life balance.

Generation X in some ways is the neglected generation. Pew Research Center labeled it as the neglected middle child of America. They are less in numbers because of the lower fertility rates seen in their parents as well as being given only 16-year range as opposed to 20-year range for every other generation. Something exceptional about the Generation X is that of all the generations, it is the only generation that was able to recover its lost wealth after the 2008–2009 housing crisis.[6] All the other generations never fully recovered their lost wealth. The Gen X population was one of the first ones to fuel the efforts that brought us into the age of computers and Internet. This was possible due to their inherent flexibility and skepticism as well as the need to be independent.

MILLENNIALS

The population that qualifies to be identified as the Millennials was born between the years 1981 and 2000. This, achievement-oriented, population will make up 75% of the total global workforce by 2025.[7] Millennials are characterized as civic and open minded. The Internet played a major role in shaping this population who were quick to adopt social technologies such as emails and text messaging. Millennials are quick to resign from corporation than their predecessors if their organization does not provide opportunities for growth and development or sufficient challenge.

Millennials seek flexibility in their schedule as well as in their work assignments. They are result driven. They also believe in work hard play harder. The tragic event of 9/11 has left a deep impression on the psyche of this generation, which has brought numerous ripple effects in the priorities of life as well as in the ways of conducting and living life. Millennials don't save much but do consider spending money extensively on travel and gathering experiences. They are also the generation that is most likely in large debts. Millennials are the backbone of many a large and major corporations globally.

GENERATION Z

Generation Z also known as Gen Z is made up of people that are born between 2001 and 2020. These individuals are digital natives. They grew up with technology, and technology has played an important role in the socialization and normative behavior development of this generation. One of the most discussed traits of this generation is their ability to focus and their duration of attention. The lack of both in Gen Z is ascribed to the uninhibited access and reckless use of smart phones and tablets. Gen Z population is a progressive generational category, which is made up of individuals that consider themselves as global citizens with progressive and entrepreneurial traits. Other than technology their life has also been shaped by the structural and systematic changes brought in the aftermath of 9/11.

Gen Z is a generation that does not like to talk on the phone. They love texting and emailing. But they are also the ones that stand up the most for climate change activism. They make excellent use of social media for advocacy and engagement with the issue. This is also a generation that is most in tune with cyber norms and behaviors. They are inseparable from their digital devices and Internet and their virtual worlds. They possess the expertise when it comes to new technologies and prefer to work with millennials as opposed to members of any other generations. They like to have multiple interactions with their bosses, which can be construed as spoon feeding by members of other generations. Gen Zers, in comparison to the other generations, know more individuals that use gender neutral pronouns.[8]

PSYCHOGRAPHIC OR MINDSET BASED

Psychographic generational categorization is a bit challenging to grasp because of its counter-intuitive nature. This form of generational categorization is based on the Maslow's Hierarchy of needs. However, there is also another concept that plays a big role in determining the categorization. There is a phenomenon known as "Cultural freezer", which is mainly used for immigrants. Immigrants hold on to traditions and rituals of their own culture from when they left their country, but the people of the nation have moved beyond those rituals and customs and in many cases even entirely forgotten them. I will employ the same logic to come up with a similar concept and name it as "Mindset Freezer". Maslow identified five different needs starting from the physiological needs such as nutrition, water, air, shelter, clothing, sleep, communication, and reproduction. Safety needs such as personal security, good health, home, property, and employment follow the physiological needs. Once these two are met the needs for love and belonging through friendship, family, belonging to groups and communities, and intimacy follow. The need for self-esteem comes next where an individual needs respect and recognition of and from the society and community. The last one is the need for self-actualization where one desires the actualization of one's total potential and fulfills the needs to be involved in creative pursuits.

In the Maslow's Hierarchy of Needs, at the base level after physiological needs is safety and security. The generations that have experienced immense lack of these needs in their formative years such as the silent generation during the great depression and WW II continue to still be frugal and saving for tomorrow. Psychologically they are still concerned about what is going to happen tomorrow. They are hyper-vigilant about securing their tomorrow. This is because they are trapped in the mindset freezer. Their actions are contradictory to their actual state of being and possession. A large majority of them today are independently wealthy, do not have to worry about their recurring bills, and have the liberty to engage in their creative pursuits. They don't do that. On the contrary, the younger generations such as the millennials and the Gen Z, which is just coming into adulthood and most of who must worry about paying bills are more liberated and living life as if they were in the self-actualization zone. Millennials and Gen Z are living freely gathering experiences while not worrying much about the bills and not saving for the future when they should. This is contradictory but based on how self-actualized individual behavior is, individuals can be categorized into different generations. Based on psychosocial and sociocultural people can be categorized into different generations.

We have often heard of the classifications of generations based on these characteristics. First-generation immigrants and third-generation immigrants are one of the most prominent examples. First-generation immigrants live like the members of the Silent Generation. They are the generation of those individuals now who have everything and still live like they have nothing. They are also loyal and grateful to the extent that they will not speak against wrongdoing just because they were first given a chance decades ago to live and prosper. The second generation is of those who have a lot more resource wise but little courage to deviate from the values set by the first generation of immigrants. They are still subservient because they try to continue and uplift, crystalize, and contextualize the values of their origin to the new space. The third-generation immigrants who themselves don't really have much in terms of resources but they live at the highest level of Maslow's pyramid. They create their own norms and embody a shift away from the subservient culture. We also hear about generations in terms of education. It could very well be a Gen Z who could be a first-generation student. And we take extra care of these students because it is not easy for them to navigate an unfamiliar territory. Technology and automobiles and other such goods too, we find the use of generations frequently. In a later chapter, I share another way to understand generations and categorize people into different generations.

THE CRISIS OF MULTIGENERATIONALITY

Multigenerationality has vast impact on all aspects of society, culture, and norms. The vast impact can be clearly seen in five macro-sectors. In the next section, I briefly highlight the impact of Multigenerationality on each of the five macro-sectors to sensitize the reader to the nature of the beast.

CORPORATES

While having multiple generations in one team lends it unique strength, the lack of harmony between them will sap the team's strength and be the reason for waste of resources and talent. Corporations are suffering because of the inherent inability to manage and navigate Multigenerationality.

For the longest time in the history of workforce and corporations, it was the norm that more experienced individuals, which was directly correlated to age, hired individuals with less experience. In other words, older people with senior positions hired younger people. This norm has not only been challenged in the age of Multigenerationality but also greatly altered. In the age of Multigenerational Convergence,[9] the ideas of where experience and expertise are housed have modified. In the era of disruptive innovation, founders such as Mark Zuckerberg who started Facebook at the age of 19 hired several employees that were of a different older generation and considering the age at which they started it is highly likely that the ones who they hired were older and more experience than them. With the increase in the disruptive, entrepreneurial and start-up culture, many innovators and founders are young in age and frequently hire employees that belong to different generations. The distance between generations obfuscates the understanding of the other individual ultimately leading to distrust toward them. Such distrust unfortunately has nothing to do with the ability and the qualifications of the person. It is due to the shroud of uncertainty that he or she or they bring by belonging to a different generation. Lack of trust and respect for one another in a corporate environment creates a toxic culture making collaboration and innovation hard to actualize.

A reason worth highlighting for the availability of members of multiple generations for the workforce is retirement age. Half a century or more ago the retirement age for an employee was not the same as it is today. With the rise in global life expectancy, the retirement age is also moving up. The threshold to receive state benefits such as pension and health care too have increased in some countries gradually and in some more steeply. In the next 20 years, the threshold is likely to be much closer to 70 years. What all this means is that older populations keep working while newer populations keep entering the workforce. People all over the globe and especially in countries like the United States are working and otherwise available for work at ages that previously would have been an anomaly. Many private corporations have provisions to retain their employees past their retirement ages.

The reader may remember a popular movie "The Intern" with Robert De Niro and Anne Hathaway as lead actors. This movie was about a retired Vice

President who was recently widowed. He had worked for 40 years, and to make good use of his time applies for a program where seniors with work experience are hired in new up and coming Internet companies as interns. As he journeys through the experience of being in an environment where everyone including the Founder and the CEO of the company is of his grandchildren's age, and in other words individuals belonging to at least two generations removed from him we get to see numerous instances of starkly different cognitive and behavior patterns. This movie beautifully highlights issues of Multigenerationality and ultimately the positive outcomes emerging from Intergenerational Harmony.

FAMILY

Family, as an enterprise, is struggling due to Multigenerationality. 2016 saw 64 million Americans cohabiting multigenerational homes.[10] And this increased during COVID. Multiple generations suddenly found themselves cohabiting. Multigenerational homes are much more common among Hispanic and Asian population than White population, and with steadily increasing Hispanic and Asian population multigenerational homes will continue to see a rise. The year and half of intense COVID has highlighted serious fault lines in the Multigenerational family living that needs to be addressed. These fault lines will eventually brutally resist multigenerational convergence and subsequent progress of civilizational enterprises and endeavors. Many Millennials and Gen Zers who left their parent's home and created a temporary nest in different cities returned home for one or more of the three reasons.

(1) Cost-efficiency – Paying rents when one does not have the same income due to job loss or income reduction made it impossible to live in big metro cities.

(2) Work from home – With enabling technologies such as Internet connectivity and ZOOM in tandem with the emergency need to not gather and meet made work from home a requisite and a reality for the future. This also pushed many closer to their families.

(3) End of Life Wisdom – For many the choice was clear that I will not die in a foreign land or a city amidst unknown and uncaring faces. If I am going to die, I will die in a village or a city where I belong and where I am surrounded by family and relatives that unconditionally love me.

Due to the mass migration, individuals who were used to living in their rented nests were now living in the homes that belonged to their parents. Living under someone else's roof requires higher ability to navigate Multi-generationality. In some advanced countries, thankfully, space was not an issue like in many developing and underdeveloped countries with high-density population. While it can be said that homes have gotten bigger, but has it led to cohesive and integrated families are the critical consideration. Although everyone is living under the same roof, everyone has their own independent existence in their separate rooms. Common and communal areas and spaces are seldom used. Such arrangement has contributed to the widening of the generational gaps. It is worth learning about the story of the Chief Financial Officer (CFO).

I was conducting a Creativity workshop for a Fortune 200 company. A lunch was organized as an extended Q&A opportunity and a deeper engagement. While having lunch, I was approached by the CFO of the company. He approached me to share his concerns about the future of his two boys and how he could utilize creativity to engage them in worthy pursuits. After listening to the concerns, I enquired about a few things, and one of them was the home in which they lived. This is when the CFO shared an interesting story, which should give you an understanding of why I say that family as an enterprise is on shaky grounds. The CFO shared that when he was the finance director, he and his family lived in a two-bedroom apartment. He noted that although everyone was busy, he would still run into his boys now and then. But when he became the CFO and started earning more salary, he bought and moved into a five-bedroom two storied apartment. He said that the real price he paid for the bigger two-storied home was that he never got to see his boys. They were home but in their respective bedrooms on a different floor. He never saw them. This affected him psychologically to the extent that he sold the big house and downsized to a smaller home where the members of the family were in some way forced to bump into or interact with one another during the day. The larger point here is whether the spaces we inhabit and the habits we have adopted are suitable for reducing issues of Multigenerationality or exacerbating it.

Introduction of newer technologies, despite its promise, is not helping in bridging the widening generational gaps. It is on the contrary creating spaces for further segregation of generations. For example, social media introduced a common platform for members of different generations to assemble and discuss topics of interest and relevance. Instead, generational segregation is observed on these platforms with greater intensity rendering these merchants of attention are data not as helpful or useful in bringing about the multigenerational convergence.

One of the reasons is that social media platform affords its users to create as many micro-bubbles and micro-spaces as possible within the larger space. Even within the same cyber architecture, one can create a safe and secure space where only a select few or chosen are allowed, and despite being within the same space, remain isolated. Allegiance and alliances to forms of technology, by themselves further solidifies generational stereotypes and encourages biases. It is becoming increasingly common to hear things like "we are an android family" or "we are an apple family". Recently, we came across an interesting story that included both smart and dumb technology. Although the story is of the intersection of technologies the real focus should be on the wide varieties and kinds of reasonable and unreasonable adjustments that people must make due to Multigenerationality in a family.

EDUCATION

A group of knowledge workers within Institutions of Higher Education such as universities hold a special distinction where they have no retirement age. The system of tenure that was initiated in Stanford University, which is now a foundational part of all universities provides a special privilege for knowledge workers to work for as long as they wish to do so. This allows for unique multigenerational convergence within the workspace.

The wave of technology in learning systems fueled systematic changes in pedagogical strategies. Introduction of Learning management systems such as Canvas and Blackboard is almost a mandatory part of every college classroom experience. Online quizzes, assignment submission, discussions, and message and information exchange mechanisms have advanced so much that it has even eradicated the need to remain physically present in a classroom. The pandemic forced online synchronous and asynchronous classrooms that were on the periphery right into the center. These changes put instructors that belong to the Baby Boomer generation and Generation X at a serious disadvantage. The same is true even for those Baby Boomers and Gen Xers who are returning as students. The surge in nontraditional students in universities has made classrooms a playground for Multigenerationality. Educational institutions these days give more prominence and spend more resources in identifying and securing a business model rather than an educational model. What are the intended and unintended learnings that become possible in a classroom that is powered by technology?

First-generation students are in the classroom with nontraditional students of a different generation resulting in a multigenerational classroom. The online classroom has further increased Multigenerationality in the learning space. Being a teacher is not as financially suitable as it was 30 years ago. There are more schools and universities and less teachers in general. There are lesser and lesser qualified and interested teachers overall. So many new universities have opened in the developing world, and many are shutting down in the developed world because they are unable to keep up with the demands of the multi-generational times.

CHURCH

Church is only a symbol for organized religion. Organized religion is going through a crisis of retention. Christianity is losing younger generation due to several reasons such as scandals, abuse, lack of being able to connect, anachronistic practices, and more. According to an estimate, there are 15 million Americans who have left Christianity between 2011 and 2021.[11] The younger generations of the West are more and more being attracted by Eastern religions and are practicing them.

Different generations respond differently to organized religion and the role of Gods in their lives. This categorization was explained to in the best possible manner by the revered professor Jagdish Sheth during a conversation. I paraphrase that conversation here. The older generations such as the Silent Generation and Baby Boomers believed in the "God loves you" paradigm. God's positionality was supreme. God was the provider. There was no safety or security outside of the community of God. People were of the mindset that no matter the struggles and challenges in life if you were alive and safe "God loved you". You didn't break the commands of God and would dare not question the authority or supremacy of God or religious institutions.

After the passage of the great depression and the world war, when the safety needs were taken care of then the "God loves you" paradigm changed to "God is with you". With the Gen X, and Millennials choosing empowerment over being marginalized, and self-identity over group identity, the religious organizations had to change their message and paradigm to "God is with you". From the supreme controller to an ally and a friend is what the gener-ational change did to the understanding and notion of God. In advanced countries, the role of the middleman such as the priest and the pastor saw a decline in its significance and relevance.

As the generation reached the level of self-actualization needs, the paradigm once again changed. The new paradigm became "God is in you". God was no more an external agent that either provided safety and security or a friendly supporter that motivated you and stood with you as you cruised on the path of progress. God was now situated within you and manifested through your will and action. Spiritual is what more Gen Z and Millennials consider themselves as opposed to being religious. The detachment from religion is due to the follies of the religions' protectors and the enhancement in wisdom but most importantly due to the upward movement through the Maslow's Hierarchy of Needs.

How will organized religion bring in more young people while keeping those already there? Multigenerationality is the biggest conundrum for the organized religion.

GOVERNMENT

Class struggles have not disappeared, but the new theory is that of generational conflict and struggles. Multigenerationality in the functioning of government is seen through the drafting of policies and the multitude of approaches and intended actions toward different situations. As noted earlier, Baby Boomers and Generation X occupy the highest number of seats in the Congress and the Senate. When the neglected child of America gets to make determinations about the future of America and other four generations, conflict is inherent. Understanding of trust, privacy, religiosity, liberal values, foreign policy, national security, and other important issues widely varies when looked at through the generational lens.

In the era of Multigenerationality, generational values and priorities clash. Such clashes prohibit legislation to move or be amended to be reflective of the multigenerational sentiment. Just as there is partisanship and bipartisanship in politics and government, similarly there is either generational schisms or Multigenerationality.

CONCLUSION

Dysfunction is not good for any institution or enterprise. Lack of understanding and insights into how to navigate Multigenerationality are damaging the five macro-sectors and our society at large. We must learn to be open to many changes for the cohesive existence and progress of the five generations. There are different strengths and agencies within each of the five age-based generations and other generational classifications. These strengths must come together for the greater benefit of humans. The crisis of Multigenerationality, if not addressed, can turn out to be a massive deterrent preventing well-being and progress of humanity.

And as the name of the chapter suggests, Multigenerationality is here to stay. It is not going to drastically disappear. As the Silent Generation becomes silent, a new generation will come forth. The coining of the name for the new generation that is coming in has already begun and it will be the generation that is born with Artificial Intelligence, Chat GPT, and who knows might make way to a generation that can go and live on Mars. It will have so many new abilities and so many new disabilities. How is this new generation going to contribute to the multigenerational conflict is yet to be seen. I reiterate here that Multigenerationality is here to stay, and it is strategically advisable to address it sooner than later. If Multigenerationality is the question, then what is the answer?

Intergenerational Harmony is the answer.

NOTES

1. Converging Media is a book by MacIntosh where the authors talk about the Convergence, types of convergence, and implications of convergence as it pertains to media.
2. "Age & Generations". Pew Research Center. https://www.pewresearch.org/topic/generations-age/. "Generational Differences in the Workplace". Purdue Global. https://www.purdueglobal.edu/education-partnerships/generational-work-force-differences-infographic/
3. https://www.pewresearch.org/fact-tank/2021/02/12/boomers-silents-still-have-most-seats-in-congress-though-number-of-millennials-gen-xers-is-up-slightly/
4. https://www.purdueglobal.edu/education-partnerships/generational-work-force-differences-infographic/
5. https://www.pewresearch.org/fact-tank/2017/03/09/led-by-baby-boomers-divorce-rates-climb-for-americas-50-population/
6. https://www.pewresearch.org/fact-tank/2018/07/23/gen-x-rebounds-as-the-only-generation-to-recover-the-wealth-lost-after-the-housing-crash/
7. Generational Differences in Workplace (infographic) (2023) Accessed through https://www.purdueglobal.edu/education-partnerships/generational-workforce-differences-infographic/
8. https://www.pewresearch.org/social-trends/2020/05/14/on-the-cusp-of-adulthood-and-facing-an-uncertain-future-what-we-know-about-gen-z-so-far-2/
9. "Convergence is the coming together of computing, internet and media in a digital environment." This is the definition provided by MacIntosh in Converging Media.

10.   https://www.pewresearch.org/fact-tank/2018/04/05/a-record-64-million-americans-live-in-multigenerational-households/
11.   Rinker, D., & Jaffarian, M. (2022). 15 million Americans have left Christianity in the past ten years. *American Beliefs Study*. Accessed through https://www.acstechnologies.com/american-beliefs/15-million-americans-have-left-christianity-in-the-past-ten-years/

2

INTERGENERATIONAL HARMONY

"The Child is the Father of the Man" is a saying that applies to the crisis of Multigenerationality in a twisted manner. The fact that the crisis of Multigenerationality is undesirable and does not require further emphasis. As seen in the previous chapter Multigenerationality, if not managed well, has deep implications on five macrosectors. Multigenerationality is an obstacle to growth and success of humanity and its institutions, be it a corporation, or a family, or a church, or education, or the government.

To counter the crisis of Multigenerationality, I propose Intergenerational Harmony (IH). This chapter highlights and illustrates the strategic significance of IH. IH is a predictor for the long-term survival and success of an enterprise. It is a massive competitive edge for an enterprise especially in the current volatile and disruptive market conditions. We are living in a historic era where although five generations are concurrently cohabiting the planet, the distance between them is increasing. The constant introduction of newer technology is a double-edge sword and has not conclusively done good or bad for IH. While having multiple generations in one team is a rare and unique strength, the lack of harmony between them is also a reason for tremendous loss of resources and talent. The strife and agony emerging from the lack of IH can prove to be fatal for an enterprise.

With the increase in stakeholders of different generations, harmony between them has become a prerequisite for the actualization of enterprise goals and targets. Schisms between the generational stakeholders result in disharmony between the stakeholders but more importantly it can also result in the degradation of quality of the products and services offered, obstructions to the smooth transition of power and authority, dissatisfaction among the prevailing members, and worst of all disintegration of the enterprise. (This chapter will illustrate specific instances of the absence of IH that led to the downfall of select enterprises within these sectors.)

WHAT IS IH?

IH is a condition where different generational stakeholders within an enterprise are working in synergy to elevate and capitalize on the strengths of one another. IH is broken down into four dimensions of the empathy, respect, trust, and honesty (ERTH) model. The four dimensions are empathy, respect, trust, and honesty. A composite measure of these or in other words the ERTH model gives an accurate assessment of the degree of presence or absence of IH within an enterprise. A sample of scales is available in Appendix 1.

ERTH model is really significant because by deploying it one can credibly get the scope and intensity of the presence or absence of IH, which provides a sound predictive framework for the survival and success of all human enterprises, and institutions within these sectors. (The chapter will also supply an easy and simple way to assess the level of IH within your enterprise.)

WHY HARMONY?

It is obvious to wonder why IH has been put forward to counter the crisis of Multigenerationality. There are other suitable action options such as collaboration, cooperation, association, alliance, and more. Harmony was selected above all these because it is the best choice.

Harmony is like the fertile soil in the river plains. Irrespective of what you plant there, it will grow. And in case if you don't plant anything it still retains its ability to support anything that wants to grow. Harmony is not an action; it is a state of being. It is a state of existence. If the different generations are in harmony with each other than whenever they choose to come together for a purpose or without a purpose, it will happen. Harmony is a state of existence where there is no continuous need to be around or collaborate with each other because of a vested interest. Harmony in its true essence goes beyond need to be together. Harmony is not a means to an end it is an end in itself.

Like every desirable thing, harmony is not easy to achieve as well. Once harmony is established, nothing is impossible. Dictionary explains harmony as 'forming a pleasing and consistent whole'. The state of harmony is a powerhouse of potentials. Wherever there is harmony, infinite potential exists. The same can be assumed for Multigenerationality as well. If there is harmony between generations then with the combined might of all generations, human civilization can achieve so much more, whereas, without IH time resources are spent only in fixing leaks and resolving conflicts.

Harmony is essentially made of up four building blocks (see Fig. 1). They are trust, respect, empathy, and honesty. A perfect balance between these four building blocks is imperative for harmony to come into being. We refer to the four building blocks as dimensions of harmony. The same dimensions are applied in the context of IH in the form of the newly developed ERTH model. Hence, the conceptual definition of IH is the balanced presence of ERTH between members of diverse generations. A disruption or reduction in one of the four dimensions will disrupt the harmony and contribute to the crisis of Multigenerationality.

A huge advantage with IH is its measurability. Measurability is advantageous because it allows for effective monitoring, evaluation, and improvement. The first big advantage of measurability is that of monitoring. Monitoring allows one to quantify the performance level and give its reader an objective insight into the performance. Based on the available quantified figures an average can be generated and can be evaluated against a desired number. In other words, the level of IH in a corporation or a family can be measured, and we can tell how much of it exists and if it meets the average or is below the average.

Since IH is measurable, it can also be monitored. This is similar to how you monitor your heart rate using a fitness tracking device. At different time intervals the level of IH can be measured, and a trend can be generated. Such monitoring helps in calibrating by identifying what is working, what is missing, or underperforming. If it is identified that the corporation is

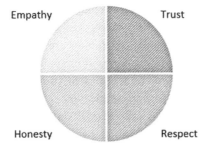

Fig. 1. Dimensions of IH.

underperforming in the area of trust, then efforts can be targeted to increase trust only.

ERTH

IH is made up of four dimensions. These four dimensions that are ERTH have been carefully chosen. Combined they form what we define as IH. IH exists only when all four are present in balanced proportions. Absence of one or lack or abundance of some are all scenarios where IH exists but it does not exist in the avatar that is most optimal in countering the crisis of Multigenerationality.

EMPATHY

Empathy enables a human being to step into the shoes of others, which is very important when navigating Multigenerationality. Nobody knows everything about everyone but with a touch of imagination and/or behavioral involvement it is possible to gain an insight into the way how members of other generations think and behave. Every generation has received different trainings in who to be and how to be. Trainings, life experiences, and availability of resources come together to influence decision-making of individuals.

Notions of loyalty have changed over the generations. Conflict in the understandings of each other leads to discrepancy and dysfunctionality between generations. In the context of family, loyalty is seen in expressions of choices pertaining to clothing, food, traditions, rituals, profession, marriage and partner choices, and more. In the corporation, there is discrepancy in the generational understanding about values, profit, and responsibility to the planet. For example, the aspect of values manifests in the understanding of people who have changed many jobs as opposed to having not changed too many jobs. Older generations do not celebrate or look positively at individuals who change too many jobs. Such employees are considered as ungrateful, fickle, and irresponsible. Younger generations are just amazed when they see individuals who have worked in a corporation for 10, 15, or 20 years. This is considered as boring behavior or worse than you are so poor in skills and devoid of ambition that no one else wants you.

Going back to family, the generational difference in understanding of monogamy is worth highlighting. In older generations monogamy meant that you spend your life with one partner, whereas now for younger generations, it means being with multiple partners over time but at any given time being with only one. With the crumbling notion of family as it existed and the birth of modern family where there are multiple sets of parents and siblings due to the making and breaking of families, loyalty obviously is not going to manifest itself as it did 50 years ago. This is where empathy comes in handy. Knowing and learning about other generations increase empathy but there is a bigger advantage to empathy.

The big advantage of empathy in navigating Multigenerationality is that it can enhance predictive ability. If you know sufficiently about one generation then you can safely guess the reaction or response to a given stimulus. Even if your guess was inaccurate, you can still leverage on your empathic intelligence to at least understand the rationale behind a response to a given situation. This becomes important in educational settings. There is incredible lack of under-standing about all the things teachers have to do for a successful 50-minute lecture. While it may vary from teacher to teacher, they still work hard to prep for the class and then finish all the grading. The same goes for students. Most college students are working one or two jobs to support themselves. The struggle of being in these time-consuming meaningless jobs and then showing interest in an 8:00 a.m. class is unknown to other generations. Empathy opens door to forgiveness.

Empathy is slightly difficult to measure, and most scales of empathy are really long making them difficult to administer and they also do not fit well in the cost-benefit equation. The length of time needed to administer made the longer scales not suitable for measuring empathy in the IH context. To overcome that challenge, the mentalizing scale was modified to the context of IH. It is a five-item scale and does a decent enough job of measuring the prevalent empathy one holds toward members of other generations. The takers can give their responses with Yes or No. For purposes of analyses, the items are scored on a 1 (Yes) and 0 (No) basis. The set of items is averaged to produce a scale score.

EMPATHY SCALE: MODIFIED FROM THE FOUR-ITEM MENTALIZING SCALE

- I find it easy to put myself in the shoes of members of other generation.

- I find it easy to see things from members of other generations' point of view.

- I think that the viewpoint of members of other generations is equally important as mine.

- I try to understand members of other generations better by imagining how things look from their perspective.

- I can usually understand members of other generations' viewpoint, even if it differs from my own.

RESPECT

In the crisis of Multigenerationality, it is often observed that members of one generation don't respect the members of other generations. Here we just want to introduce respect, provide a brief rationale for its inclusion as one of the dimensions, and then touch upon its measurement. Respect is not a linear or a simple construct. There are different needs and nuances of respect in respect with different generations. Respect is largely related with other variables of self-esteem and involvement.

Some generations, mainly older, expect respect for their existence, whereas younger generations do not expect that. They, on the contrary, expect respect for their ideas and choices. In a different chapter, we will provide a much more detailed understanding of respect along with strategies to build and increase respect. Privilege and entitlement are two other notions that are related to the expectation of and giving of respect. Achievements of and by a generation also play a role in the expectation of respect. For example, it is common to hear that we are the generation who lived through the great depression, and we were the ones who fought the wars and shed blood that is enabling you to live the free and independent life that you are living, and for it you should be thankful to us and respect us. While this argument makes sense on the face value, it does not automatically warrant the granting of unconditional respect because members of other generations look at it from a different point of view. Their counterargument is that your generations waged all the wars and killed so many innocent humans. Waging war and killing innocent is not something that is worthy of respect. This is where empathy plays a role, and you will read a bit more about the cross-sectionality of empathy and respect.

In addition to empathy, knowledge about other generations and their struggles, accomplishments, etc. also play a role in the fostering of respect. The presence or absence of hierarchy also enables or disables respect. In religious settings, individuals who are in the position of a priest or a pastor automatically get a certain level of respect, and the same goes for principals and teachers and professors in the educational settings.

There are several existing valid and reliable scales for measuring respect. And the readers are free to create their own as well. However, the one that I found and would like to suggest is the Respect toward other Generations Scale. The scale consists of 5 Yes or No items/questions. The Respect toward Partner Scale was modified and adapted to the needs of IH for creating this scale. The reason why this scale was chosen is that it is simple and easy to administer as well as measure. It also does justice to measuring and assessing the prevalent level of respect one has toward members of other generations. And they are provided below.

RESPECT TOWARD OTHER GENERATIONS SCALE

- I respect members of other generations.

- I am interested in members of other generations as persons.

- I am a source of healing for members of other generations.

- I honor members of other generations.

- I communicate well with members of other generations.

TRUST

Trust is integral to collaboration. The crisis of Multigenerationality exacerbates immensely if we are unable to build trust between generations. In a later chapter, the reader will learn about rebuilding trust between different generations. But at the moment we will focus on the giving a brief introduction to areas where lack of trust is most likely leading to dysfunctionality.

Lack of trust in clergy due to the large number of scandals pertaining to abuse of power has brought about great dysfunctionality in the church. The lack of trust became worse when people learned that the church itself saved the clergy from the justice system. This was a double blow for the followers.

In education system, the lack of trust in the instructor of a precomputer era generation to be able to deliver a lecture which can add value to the student is an area of concern. The nature and notion of life-long skills is seriously being challenged by the wave-like nature of technology. Just as waves keep hitting the shores of a beach, new technology also keeps entering our lives. This is increasing the gap between the skills and lessons taught in classrooms in relation with the ones that are needed to succeed and survive in the new age technological world. This discrepancy corrodes trust at a level where recovery becomes demanding.

The modern family is riddled with inconsistencies and uncertainties. While in many places, parents heave a sigh of relief when their daughter escapes teenage pregnancy, at the same time children also celebrate if, by the time they graduate high school, their parents remain together. The choice of framing between new age families and broken families is critical because it has to do with the underlying trust a member of the family has on other generational members of family. "Your generation has everything and all the opportunities that we did not" is a common dialog heard in households. Erosion of trust in the generational constants of family has near eliminated a blanket of security and comfort.

We modified the general trust scale to fit the needs of IH and suggest a five-item scale for measuring trust. The trust scale is again a Yes/no. The score for each item is averaged to calculate a measure of generalized trust.

TRUST SCALE: MODIFIED FROM THE GENERAL TRUST SCALE

- Most members of other generations are basically honest.
- Most members of other generations are trustworthy.
- Most members of other generations are basically good and kind.
- Most members of other generations are trustful of others.
- Most members of other generations will respond in kind when they are trusted by others.

HONESTY

The perception of the level of honesty that other generations demonstrate toward your generations plays a huge role in IH. Without honesty there is no harmony. Dishonesty will only erode trust, deplete respect, and further aggravate the crisis of Multigenerationality. Dishonesty is not to be construed as lying but also to be seen as the manifestation of behaviors and policies that systematically eliminates the benefits of a given generation.

Earlier I referred to church and the tragedy its followers had to endure. The clergy who misused and abused their power to prey on members of younger generations have done a lasting damage to followers. This was a demonstration of lack of respect that some clergy men had for members of other generations. But the systematic suppression of the scandalous behavior and protection of such clergy was a demonstration of dishonesty by the church. Hypocrisy in the practicing of beliefs and traditions that emanate from religions by the generations that preach it and the generations from whom the expectation is of adhering to is another example of dishonesty.

Not allowing members of other generations to grow within government and corporations is another way of lack of honesty manifests. Passing legislations that promote benefits to a certain group and leaving others behind is yet another example. Restricting flow of information or indulging in selective information dissemination is also a dishonest practice that sows seeds of distrust and generational conflict. Honesty, unfortunately, does not come easily or naturally to most. To cultivate honesty, one needs to create an internal milieu of peace and silence where one is able to receive the needed clarity to discern what is honest and truthful and what is not.

Every university has policies and people to enforce, mitigate, and eradicate issues of academic integrity. All forms of shortcuts that are adopted to get more marks or a better grade without actually digesting any learning are manifestations of dishonesty. Who gets most affected by cheating in an exam. A student or an instructor? The same goes for Government too. It spends so many resources to curb dishonesty in the very many aspects of civic living. Absolute honesty, although appealing, can be construed as unemotional and inconsiderate. This is why different generations draw different lines for what is honest and what is not.

Storytelling is one of the biggest breeding grounds for dishonesty between generations. I say so because if this were not the case, religious texts, if you think rationally, came into existence to avoid dishonest contamination. Humanity relied on oral traditions. This was true for many until four centuries ago, but it is true for some even today. There was no way to discern whether alterations in storytelling and iterations of it were intentional or unintentional. Compromises in honesty likely led to the need for standardization. Hence the religious text was created. But the realm of dishonesty did not end with it because now it is a tug-of-war between which interpretation is the honest one. The divide between the Catholics and the protestants is due to the argument about which interpretation or extant understanding is the honest and accurate one.

In the crisis of Multigenerationality, honesty is truly the game changer. Trust and respect would become easier if there was a prevailing conviction that the members of other generations are honest. This can be measured by the modified honesty scale, which was modified from the honesty scale that used to explore the threat posed by copycats who pretend to be something but are not.[1] The modified honesty scale is made up of five items and the respondents use Yes or No responses.

HONESTY SCALE: MODIFIED FROM HONESTY SCALE

- I believe what members of other generations say.

- Members of other generations have integrity.

- I trust members of other generations will tell me the truth.

- Members of other generations are honorable.

- Members of other generations are honest.

MEASURING IH QUOTIENT WITH ERTH

As discussed previously, a major advantage of IH is its measurability. IH is a composite score of the four dimensions of ERTH. There is no direct measure of IH, and therefore we are resorting to measuring it by first measuring the four dimensions and then adding up their aggregate scores to arrive at a score of IH. The score of IH quotient ranges from a minimum score of 0 and a maximum score of 20. Stars are assigned for every four points. Table 1 provides a clear understanding for allocating stars based on the score. A star symbol is used for the IH quotient. We use the star symbol to understand and interpret the level of IH. The 5-star symbol system is a fairly popular way of understanding quality and hence has been adopted for its cognitive ease and visual benefits.

But to get to that first the reader must utilize the four suggested scales and deploy them among the participant population. Once the scores from the four dimensions of ERTH, which are honesty, trust, respect, and empathy, are collected from all the participants they can be averaged, and the resulting aggregate score serves as the IH quotient of a given population. The ERTH

Table 1. Star Allocation System.

IH Quotient	Number of Stars
0	0
1–4	1
5–8	2
9–12	3
13–16	4
17–20	5

score will give you an indication of what is the level of harmony that exists between the generations within a given population. Table 2 gives an understanding of the interpretation of stars and IH scores.

Once the stars are allocated, then one can refer to the reference guide provided in the Table 2 to get a broad overview of the level of IH in the respective human enterprise. As evident from Table 2, the IH scores are absolute scores. Although they are useful to understand the level of IH between different generations, and they do inform the enterprise about the need for improvement, they do not inform much about specific areas of improvement.

If based on the above interpretation, a need for some form of intervention is established then the next step is to identify which of the four dimension is struggling. For this we go back to the results of the scales of four dimensions and chart them using the color gradient-based system. For each dimension, there is a triangle and they all come together tangentially at the center point. Once again, the highest score for any dimension can be 5 or the lowest possible score could be 0. A gradient-based representation of the results is presented in Fig. 2, which is referred to as the Dimensional Cross.

Each triangle in the Dimensional Cross corresponds to one color. It is easy to create the Dimensional Cross. Create a triangle and then using the fill function fill it with red color. Then using the format function choose the gradient fill option. Choose the percentage based on the score you have. If you have a score of 4 then set the gradient fill at 80%, if you have a score of 3 then make it 60%, if you have a score of 2 then choose 40%, and if you have a score of 1 then choose 20%. It is highly unlikely to get the scores of 0 or 5.

The colors are important. The green-colored triangle corresponds to respect. The yellow triangle corresponds to the score of trust. The purple triangle corresponds to the dimension of empathy. And the blue triangle

Table 2. Star Reference Guide.

IH Aggregate Score	Interpretation
★☆☆☆☆	This means that there is the no harmony between the generations of this population. The environment is toxic for intergenerational collaboration and could require a complete mindset overhaul for things to change. This may be a multiyear project with numerous targeted interventions. This rating means that the crisis of Multigenerationality at its peak within a given enterprise.
★★☆☆☆	This means that there is something that is naturally working well. This could be more due to a favorable interpersonal connection as opposed to IH. This is where a large majority of enterprises would find themselves.
★★★☆☆	This is a zone where a decent minority of enterprises would find themselves upon examination. If proper and targeted action is not taken, the enterprise sinks further to suffer the effects of the crisis of Multigenerationality. Inaction is the worst for this group of enterprises.
★★★★☆	This is a desirable zone to be in and it's an indication of existing IH. Additionally, it is also an indication of potential for more harmony to be included easily. With a few short-term interventions, the enterprise can be pushed further up. This zone represents the need for little improvements and adjustments as opposed to all the ones above it.
★★★★★	This is the ideal situation for IH. In such optimal environments collaboration between generations is easy, quick, and so natural that it is a given. This needs to be studied as a best example and be shared with other aspiring enterprises. This is seldom found.

corresponds to the dimension of honesty. In addition to the four colors, the Dimensional Cross with the red color is in the background. You ideally want to see less of red and more of other colors. Let us take the Dimensional Cross presented in Fig. 2 as a case study to understand the dimensional needs for enhancing IH.

Before you start studying the Dimensional Cross in Fig. 2, take a look at Table 2. One of the rows is highlighted. For this case, we will take that row as the absolute score of IH within our example population. Three stars are highlighted and two are blank. This rating/scoring means that the enterprise is on the fence. Without immediate intervention, it risks further disharmony

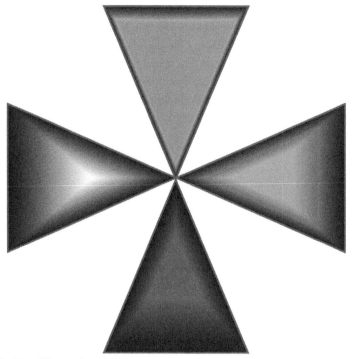

Fig. 2. The Dimensional Cross.

ultimately leading to the crisis of Multigenerationality. A rating of three is indicative of the need for intervention and improvement. But from that rating what is unclear is the dimension in which the intervention and improvement are needed. To get that information, we now refer to the Dimensional Cross in Fig. 2.

This should immediately indicate that the Trust dimension is the one that is missing the most among the four dimensions. Another dimension where the red color dominates is the purple dimension. This implies that the generations within this population are struggling with empathy as well. The color red is the dominating the least in the dimension that corresponds to the green color. And this is the dimension of respect. It means that there is high level of respect between members of different generations. Based on the visual representation, it becomes clear for the enterprise on what aspect should it focus its targeted efforts on.

In this particular case, the enterprise needs to focus and prioritize on rebuilding trust. To do so it can choose learnings from the book on garnering IH on rebuilding trust and apply it. One singular intervention is never enough to get the desired results. Notions like trust take time and consistent effort to build over time. Once a few targeted interventions on trust are executed, the enterprise should then initiate in developing empathy between the generations. Like this depending on where the need is, different concoctions of interventions should be executed to reach at the desired level of IH.

CONCLUSION

IH is a powerful predictor of an enterprise's success in the long run. Stereotypes pertaining to other generations will need to systematically be identified, challenged, and eliminated by executing interventions in the ERTH. ERTH, by now, you would know stands for empathy, respect, trust, and honesty. IH is a prerequisite for enterprises to thrive in the present and in the time to come.

IH is a state of existence. It is a state of being with countless potentialities. The benefit of IH is that it can be measured and assessed. Upon learning about the IH quotient, it can be looked more microscopically in the Dimensional Cross to target the dimensions with strategic interventions to bring up scores in the specific dimensions. The fact that IH can be improved upon makes it a useful construct and a powerful antidote to the crisis of Multigenerationality.

NOTE

1. Reysen, S., & Puryear, C. (2014). Victims' reactions to the interpersonal threat to public identity posed by copycats. *Interpersona*, *8*, 100–114.

3

EDUCATION

Generational clashes in the domain of education are becoming more and more unpleasant. This is driving generational schisms steeper. The reasons are simple and staring at us if we choose to look at them.

I would like to begin by informing you that the cost of earning a degree has gone up by approximately 1,200% in comparison to 1980s.[1] Between the three generations that have studied and learned and earned degrees, the financial cost that the former had to pay is astronomically lower than the latter. Research also suggests that more than 50% undergrads rely on federal aid.[2] While the available support from the state and federal government too has gone down greatly the support (federal aid) that is available for students to be able to afford education has unfortunately proved to be detrimental in the long run for members of BIPOC and other minority communities. And lastly, the degree that you get now will not guarantee you a job with stability or a remuneration that can always sustain a family. In short for the generation that wants to get educated now, the four-edged sword is cutting you deep.

The cost, opportunity, and availability of life-long education is very different for the current generation than it was for the previous generations. The notion that Education is a "short-term transactive investment" has made home in the minds and hearts of the younger generation. To be a bit sarcastic and exaggerated here, the idea of investment is so deeply rooted in kids that they come to me and ask for a 120 out of 100 as their grade. When I ask why, they say that stock markets give us 115 back for every 100 we put in, you must give us atleast 120 for every 100 that we put in. I often don't want to be the person who tells them that forget getting 115 back, a large majority of people don't even get their 100 back from the stock market.

Let us not trivialize the situation of these kids as well and instead look at life from their point of view. For most Gen Zs, education begins with incurring debts. More sadly, those who have benefitted from when the cost of education was 1,200% lower are the ones that are leading educational institutions and being responsible for teaching and giving degrees to the students of today. While there is a small group of educators who study issues of affordability and access to education, and have the needed sensitivity, a very large portion of educators just feel that something is amiss without realizing the gravity of the situation or doing anything about the situation.

Going back to the point that most Gen Zs begin by incurring debts. Forget saving any money when they start earning because the first decade or more after education is spent in repaying their debt. Please be aware that when a young person starts this journey, their brains are not fully developed to imagine the life-long cost of Education. Since a major chunk of your income goes in repaying your debt, an individual incurs more debt for acquiring a car, a home, and other related accessories. By the time an individual repays all this, they are looking to encash their social security check. Unless played wisely, education for this generation becomes the biggest and worst gamble of their life, and therefore even a liability. What if the technology you invested in financially, cognitively, and timewise becomes obsolete? Learning is not easy at an advanced age. Evolution has not yet caught up to our perennial need for learning new skills. Gradual and marginal learning is still manageable but an entire rehaul takes a toll. Humans are still not yet programmed to endure such transformation. Singapore might be the first country that attempts this at a scale. Singaporean government might subsidize a second degree in Artificial Intelligence for all their citizens above 40 to ensure that they can keep up with the changes in ecosystem.

I await the day when there will be a reality show similar to Shark Tank where there will be individuals selling their own self and asking for tuition amount as loans from the Sharks. The Sharks, in return, would get a 10% stake in the salary they earn after graduating. Depending on your past scores and future potential, Sharks will throw you in an offer for covering entirely or a portion of your tuition. When they graduate, these students will be bound by contracts to work for the companies owned or operated by these Sharks and their affiliates.

Let us take a little pause to do some reflective work before proceeding any further. I have two questions that will hopefully allow you to look at the mountain from different sides. My request to you, my dear reader, is to try to be as rational and objective as possible. Before you do so, to help stir your reflection and thinking, here is a little food for thought.

Imagine the availability, prevalence, efficiency, and ability of technology in the 1960s in comparison to the 2000s. It may not be much of a stretch to say that we are looking at two extremes. For an individual who has enjoyed an illustrious 35 year long career in education as a teacher, these would be the years when he or she or they would be at the peak of their wisdom and knowledge. These would be the teachers whose classes would be standing room only. If you need a little help to visualize, imagine Prof. Albert Einstein or Prof. Isaac Newton at the age of 60. How students must flock to get a glimpse of him and listen to his words of wisdom. Well now imagine the same individuals struggling with learning management systems such as Canvas and Blackboard, without which, education or a student's learning experience is incomplete. Sad, isn't it?

Now please take 5–10 minutes to think deeply and answer the question below.

Q1: What is a 60-year-old teacher CAPABLE of teaching a 20-year-old student in 2024 to progress and succeed in life?

_____

_____

_____

_____

_____

_____

_____

_____

Great job with giving it your best to respond to the first question. Take more space if you need it. While your creative juices are actively flowing, please use the next 5–10 minutes to answer the second question given below.

Q2: What is a 60-year-old teacher INCAPABLE of teaching a 20-year-old student in 2024 to progress and succeed in life?

_____

_____

_____

_____

_____

_____

_____

_____

Thank you for attempting the above two questions with your utmost objectivity and rationality as possible. Hopefully, thinking about these two questions should have given you a self-reflected glimpse into the issues of Multigenerationality in education.

Researchers, Mariano Sanchez and Matthew Kaplan,[3] make a strong case for Multigenerational Classrooms due to the increasing intergenerationality. They emphasize on being cognizant of the generational commonalities and differences that coexist for developing a transformational learning experience. Important to note is that outside of the learning environment, individuals of different generations cross paths to sustain the social, cultural, commercial tenets of civilization. Diversity, albeit generational diversity or multi-generationality hence must be a cornerstone of education.

Just as how the sprawling suburbia is giving rise to human-animal conflicts, similarly, with the exploding age diversity in education, especially in higher education, generational conflicts have become a point of contention in the world of education. Seeking education and learning is interminable. It is encouraged in all phases of life in turn bringing all new types and kinds of students into the classroom. In addition to the age-based diversity, there is also a geography-based diversity. A classroom has become much more heterogenous geographically than before. This is especially true of and high in the online asynchronous formats of teaching. A large online course offered by a Harvard or Stanford Professor through e-learning platforms such as edX will have students enrolled in it from countless geographies with varying demographics. As long as they have a stable internet, they are good to go.

It is not uncommon to have a 55-year-old plumber from Kazakhstan participating in an online course in the middle of the night offered by a faculty that is 20 years younger to him or her or them based in Idaho. More and more students that are in their thirties and forties are turning to education. They are, in many ways, compelled by the substantially decreased utility-based expiry date of educational degrees. Half a century ago, if you got a degree in a field, you could continue to work in the field for the rest of your life with little to no updating. However, that is not the case now. New fields are coming in, new job roles are coming in, and it is likely that all your education as recent as seven years ago is obsolete. Hence if you completed your masters at the age of 23–24, then by the time you are 30, it will be likely that you may need to go back to school for micro-credentials or fully new credentials. European Union saw an increase of 55% in the number of students that are aged 40 and higher in just a decade.[3] Researchers of the same study further note that in the US in 2011, 56% students were the non-traditional students. Or in other words not between the age of 18–24. The surge in non-traditional students in universities has made classrooms a playground for Multigenerationality.

A group of knowledge workers within institutions of higher education such as universities hold a special distinction where they have no retirement age. The system of tenure that was initiated in Stanford University, which is now a foundational part of all universities provides a special privilege for knowledge workers to work for as long as they wish to do so with immunity against backlash from administration for conducting research and advancement of knowledge. This system allows for unique multigenerational convergence within the workspace. While it has enabled research to proliferate well, it has created some issues on the teaching front. The wave of technology in learning systems has fueled systematic changes in pedagogical strategies. Introduction of learning management systems such as Canvas and Blackboard are almost a mandatory part of every college learning experience. Online quizzes, assignment submission, discussions, and message and information exchange mechanisms have advanced so much that it has even eradicated the need to remain physically present in a classroom. The pandemic forced online synchronous and asynchronous classrooms that were on the periphery right into the center. These changes put instructors that belong to the Baby Boomer generation and Generation X at a serious disadvantage. The same is true even for those baby boomers and Gen Xers who are returning as students. In sum, education has become an incredibly hostile playground for the crisis of multigenerationality.

ATTENTION, CURIOSITY, AND ENGAGEMENT AND SOME OTHER SELECTED ISSUES WORTH MENTIONING

In the year 2022–2023, I visited more than 60 institutions of learning and education in the country of India. During my visits, I interacted with thousands of students, teachers, and administrators located in urban, rural, and tribal settings of the vast and highly populous country. I saw Multigenerationality, exacerbated by COVID-19 pandemic, in action causing deep fissures in the ethos and fabric of learning and education. Upon my return to the US and being interwoven with the world of education as an academic, I noticed a distinct set of challenges emerging in education from Multigenerationality. In no particular order, I want to share my observations, my concerns, my reflections and my subjective interpretations about selected issues that I find worth including here.

Globally, educators face the issues of dampening attention, curiosity, and engagement among their students. Lack of attention was the most common complaint in every teaching institution that I visited. All the teachers that I have interacted in different countries of North America, South America, Europe, Asia, and Australia have expressed their anguish and frustration over this issue. Educators all over the world believe that attention is the strongest ally of an educator. If an educator is able to capture the attention of his or her or their students, then they can easily transfer learnings to them.

Another major issue is of the absence of curiosity. There is so much over-exposure that children are hardly ever curious. Before a teacher can introduce the magical concepts of solar system or dinosaur, kids have already seen documentaries about it and played with toy versions or video game versions of it. It is challenging to come across a virgin learner. Parents too in their hurry to ensure that their kid is ahead of the curve expose them to so many things. Now mere exposure to new concepts and things eventually results in the dampening of curiosity. Curiosity is a driver of attention. Hence, introduction to certain topics and concepts has to be done using proper pedagogical techniques so that fascination and curiosity about that concept remains ingrained in the psyche of the learner. Parents, by default, don't have extensive training in pedagogy. And I believe, it was therefore very rare for me all throughout my visits to see kids walking into their schools with curiosity. Instead, it was commonplace to see them walk in with the combined burden of stress, leth-argy, and melancholy.

I also noticed that a multigenerational perspective as well as multigenera-tional sensitivity is missing in this piece of the puzzle. A large majority of current teachers and educators come from the so-called prehistoric era of no cell phones. But it was not that they were completely unhooked. They were hooked on to video games or TV or radio or comic books. However, all these could very easily be regulated and restricted by parents, unlike cellphones. When I say that I find the multigenerational sensitivity or perspective missing, what I mean is that everyone continues to lament the absence of attention and curiosity in children instead of working with it. There is absolutely no way this trend can be reversed. There is no way that the next generation can be dis-allowed electronic devices or streaming services. So now instead of lamenting, we should actively start working on redesigning pedagogies and curricula for students with little to no attention and curiosity. How does the same topic need to be taught if someone is disinterested, and inattentive? Accepting this reality and working with this approach would be a healthy example of generational synergy. But such generational synergy can only come into play if there is intergenerational harmony. It is only when we look at the other person not as a source of agony and anguish but as a source of fascination and challenge that a synergized change can be brought.

Let's look at the same mountain from another side. In a recent Gallup Poll, where thousands of kids were asked to rate their schools, unsurprisingly kids scored their schools' ability to make them excited about learning with a score of C+. When I was doing my doctoral studies, I was told that anything below B for a doctoral student was actually an F. Many majors don't allow students in their major if they have a C+. Should schools and universities be allowed to run if they have a C+ in their ability to excite students about learning. I mean what else do these institutions exist for. The single point agenda common to all learning institutions is to excite students about learning and impart knowledge. And if they are failing in that then it is very hard to argue against a certain group of politicians and industrialists who are determined to destroy the very foundation of educational institutions.

From the student's point of view, they feel that their teachers are boring. I was categorized as boring too but there was something that got me out of that category. And this is worth knowing because it came as an utter shock and surprise to me. It was when some students realized that there was an "About" page on Google about me. Many of my readers may not even know what this "About" page is, neither did I. I can promise that not a single teacher on the planet would have ever realized that the way to not be categorized as boring did not involve earning a master's degree or a doctoral degree or years of teaching experience or awards of excellence or years of sleepless nights. Those are all just things you hang on a wall to decorate your office space and make yourself feel good. Instead, all that was required was to have an "About" page on Google. This is the paradox and the irony of the 21st century that students think you are a cool teacher not by your teaching performance but by having an "About" page on Google about you.

I firmly feel that the students' overall perception that their teachers are boring is also intergenerationally insensitive. It is practically impossible for your teacher to be the hero or the heroine of a show you watch on streaming services. If your teacher were that ruthless or promiscuous or swore as frequently in a classroom, he or she or they would not have a job from the very next day. There isn't a team of 200 people working and constantly ideating about how to make your next class on photosynthesis or probability or solar system as exciting as the launch of the next iPhone. I so wish that educational institutions had budgets and human resources that equaled if not surpassed the budgets of movies and streaming shows and iPhone launches. Actually, why do we not have that? We should. Otherwise, we are entering the boxing ring with our hands tied. Nonetheless, to expect that your teacher can create the same level of excitement as your streaming shows is unreal, and generationally insensitive.

Again, let us try to look at the mountain from another side. Personally, I don't believe that there is a problem with attention at all. I on the contrary feel that we are living in an era where our attention span has extended beyond imagination. Sleep is the most precious thing for humans. We have to pay people extra if they are going to sacrifice their sleep to work when it's time to sleep. Most of the major decisions our civilization makes are kept keeping sleep and meals in mind. Despite its immense significance, there is a large portion of humanity today that is willingly sacrificing their sleep every day. They are doing so to watch reels or shows. People are sacrificing their sleep but paying rapt attention to their media. An utterly unhealthy term "binge" is now commonplace in media behavior. It is common to hear people speak of how they binged on a show and stayed up the entire night. This was while paying full attention. So, if you think about this from my twisted and creative point of view, attention spans have increased to upwards of 10 hours. But when it comes to paying attention in a classroom or a learning environment, we can't even reach upwards of 10 seconds. While teachers can imbibe some aspects of storytelling from shows and movies and reels, but they simply cannot get your attention in 5 seconds and your tendency to press the mental skip button is just so beyond your control that you succumb to it. Students should be mindful that not every teacher or professor they come across can be like Jon Snow or Don Draper or Chandler Bing or Emily in Paris or DCI Cassie Stuart.

Moreover, I also realized and learned that lack of attention, curiosity, and engagement are not only due to electronic devices and streaming media content. These kids are pretty much born with these devices, so for them it is what water is for a fish. Let me share the instance that alerted me to the fact that there are many other, some expected and some completely unexpected, reasons for the lack of attention, curiosity, and engagement. While teaching one day in the US, I noticed that there was an overall lethargy and melancholy in the class. Students being tired and uninterested is not a surprise. But this day it was a bit more than usual. So, I took a pause from teaching, sat down in front of them, and asked them with utmost concern I could visibly demonstrate on my face, "What do you need to be happy?"

The first student said, "Sleep, I could do with some more sleep." Second student said, "Time. I would be happy if I had more time." I looked at the third student and they said, "Food". "What do you mean by food?" I countered immediately. "Well, I haven't had anything to eat since morning. I directly woke up for my class and then I didn't have time, so I haven't eaten until now." A bit puzzled, I asked, "But our class starts at 2:30. Are you telling me that you woke up at 2 pm and rushed here?" They replied saying that they had another class at 10 a.m. so they have been awake since then. Upon probing a bit more, I learned that the student does not have money to feed themself and often goes for days only on one meal. They do not have enough money despite working four jobs to have two meals every day of the month. I am not suggesting that there have not been students who come from an impoverished background in the past. We are still not being able to feed our students in the 21st century in the most advanced and powerful nation in the world is the unfortunate reality. What kind of attention, curiosity, and engagement can you expect from a hungry young kid?

What another student told me flummoxed me. This another student said, "since the 2016 presidential elections their family has been torn apart. One half of the family hails President Trump as God and the other half wants to burn him alive. There has been such extreme polarization in the family that we have not had a proper thanksgiving or Christmas celebration since then. And I am just tired of this brokenness and bitterness among my family. I want the bickering and back-biting to stop as it is toxic and distressing." This left me dumbstruck. Once again, what kind of attention, curiosity, and engagement can you expect from a distressed kid?

Sleeplessness, hunger, mental health, learning disabilities, sexual harassment and abuse, relationship troubles, family problems, bullying, obsessive consumption of mass and social media, and affordability are, in my humble opinion, also the reasons for the lack of participation and enthusiasm of students in the class. While I observed more and more hunger among students, at the same time, I also saw massive programs such as "Anganwadis" in India that bring millions of children to school by promising and feeding them healthy meals, which their parents cannot otherwise afford to provide. There are government run programs, which provide education, boarding, and food to tribal children. For tribal or rural girls, there is an even more special program run in India. If a family has a girl as an elder child and then if they give birth to a boy then the girl's education is discontinued, and instead of her the boy will be sent to school. Indian government runs a special program where they identify such girls and bring them with the consent of their parents to take specially designed tests. These tests allow the authorities to deduce the right school age. The girl is then provided all free facilities to study, live, eat, and more and encouraged to pass the basic matriculation exam. The Indian government takes care of all the costs, which was initially the main reason why the girl was deprived of education. I have visited such a school facility. And it is heartwarming to see girls, who were forgotten and neglected, being given a fair chance. So, while I see terrific efforts to educate the most unreachable, I also see lethargy in keeping the ones that are already enrolled in.

For the Upward Bound program of the US Department of Education, I taught Math for a semester to 8th and 9th grade at-risk students from dangerous urban neighborhoods. These urban kids too don't pay attention and are, if one is to stereotype, some of the unruliest kids. The aim of the program is to keep students out of streets and prevent them from being poached by street gangs. The life circumstances and issues plaguing them are unimaginable. Without intergenerational harmony we will only distance them. We have to have the needed generational synergy to integrate these kids into mainstream. I distinctly remember this one student, who was super sweet and caring toward everyone around her. She was not at all good in her studies but as a human, she was the best. One day she was unusually quiet and not herself. I asked her what the reason was and with the saddest face she replied that previous night her boyfriend was arrested for being involved in a gun fight, and she has not had a conversation with him in the past 14 hours due to which she was worried about him and could not focus. This too is the reality of kids in urban at-risk areas. An 8th grader missing a boyfriend. Is this a generational issue? Moreover, there was one thing similar between every kid who was in my class that semester. They all came from broken families or modern families, whichever framing you find most suitable.

I also want to highlight another issue that does not often get any airspace. And to some extent I don't know if this even qualifies as an intergenerational issue, but I am going to go ahead and atleast mention it. You can decide if it's a generational thing or not. As an instructor I can vouch for the fact that there is not one time slot in the 24 hours, where you enter a class and students are not tired and uninterested. Morning is too soon, afternoon is lunch hour, late afternoon is lethargic due to the lunch hour, evening is tiresome because one has spent so many hours awake, and night is to relax, consume food for the body, and watch reels.

Similarly, there is not one ideal day of the week for studying or coming to the class. Monday is when you are tired from a relaxing weekend, Tuesday is when you are waking up, Wednesday, one is already tired of it being the hump day, Thursday brings with it some excitement because one can go to the bar to start planning the weekend, and Friday one is in no mood because weekend has started. While this may be oversimplifying and over generalizing but there is no day and time when education is a priority.

Relevance is a concept that is also at the heart of attention and curiosity and also engagement. If a person believes that something is relevant to them, they are naturally more inclined to pay attention and be curious and even engage with the person and the topic. Is what is happening in our learning environments generationally relevant? Are our modes of teaching and topics of teaching relevant are some questions one needs to ask for building stronger generational synergy. I am sharing two cases below to help you further ponder about the relevance aspect.

Case 1

Jack is a junior in high school in the rural mid-west of America. He aspires to become an influencer. He has already started putting actions in that direction where he runs his own YouTube Channel and has acquired 41k followers. His monthly income from ad revenues is averaged at $2500. His followers too are young like him. Youngsters are the favorite target audience for countless new age brands who are all trying to follow the age-old mantra of 'catch them young'. So, he has become an important mediator in the 2-step model of influencing consumers through him by affiliating with him. Jack has openly confessed that he does not care much for what happens in the classroom. And his reasoning is that everything that we are being taught is outdated and is not pertinent and he will not use any of it in his life. Moreover, he finds his teachers boring, who just drawls. Hence, he disengages and instead doodles or thinks about other things.

Case 2

Mrs. Maxwell is a teacher in the same mid-western rural high school as Jack. She is an influencer and likes to make the distinction that she is a real-life influencer because she is influencing lives of her students in real life. She has a following of 35 students who are in her class every day. Interestingly, if the students were given a choice that number would dwindle greatly. Her monthly income from her work at school is $4000. She feels that history is important and that everything that happens every day is pertinent to the lives of her students. She finds her students to be unenthused and suffering from privilege inspired apathy. She desperately tries to engage them by doing the same thing over and over again.

How do you objectively evaluate relevance in these two scenarios? I am certain that you can empathize and sympathize with both at the same time. But what do they do and what can they do? Let me identify one more issue before wrapping up this section.

The emergence of different education boards is a new change in the educational paradigm. In India, there is the central board of education. This is managed by the Center and all the schools across India affiliated with it have the same syllabi, co-curricular and extracurricular activities, timings, exam structures, and more. In addition to the central board, every state has its own respective state board of education. The state boards have different syllabi, co-curricular and extracurricular activities, timings, exam schedules, and more. Now on top of these two, we also have an International board. I am sure that there are one or two more boards of accreditations within the country.

All these have different requirements, pedagogies, and schedules. It is highly unlikely for students to be alike when they graduate from different boards in terms of their skill sets, confidence, and self-efficacy. The values imparted, exposure provided, quality of teachers is all very different in all these. By the time a child that clears his or her 10th grade or equivalent to sophomore in high school, a child from the international board would have traveled to atleast two countries as part of the school's learning experience. The child would also have participated in national competitions and traveled within the nation. The child would have been exposed to latest technologies in the school and would be university ready. Whereas a child from a state board would not have had the same experience. So once in the university their adjustment challenges are steeper and stacked more against them than other boards. However, to get admission in the international boards, one requires a substantial amount of money which most middle class, lower-middle class parents cannot afford. This phenomenon has its own sets of short- and long-term issues and troubles but let us not concern ourselves with any more than the generational ones.

Note that these are only a few major ones. There are many other observations which I have encountered during my travels and trainings. I have not included them because they don't directly fall within the scope of this book. However, there is one more, it is a big one, Technology. So, I have a separate section for it later in this chapter.

GENERATIONAL LEARNING MANTRAS

Upon careful reflection, it became evident to me that humanity, in some crooked manner, is coming a full circle when it comes to generational mantras of learning and education. Based on which generation you belong to; you can easily identify the mantra (See Fig. 3) of your generation or vice versa too is also possible.

■ Ignorance is Bliss   ■ Knowledge is Power

■ Remembering is Obsolete ■ Retrieval is the Key

■ Ignorance is Bliss

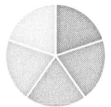

Fig. 3. Generational Learning Mantras.

IGNORANCE IS BLISS

It all begins with bliss. And ironically it all also ends with bliss. Ignorance ruled over humankind with a tight fist. This was the era of very limited knowing. Satisfaction with not knowing was not shamed or looked down upon. Remnants of this system are still seen in some mindsets that discriminate against females to force ignorance down their throats. Ignorance was also systematically and systemically propagated. Those who attempted to ward off the evils of ignorance were struck down brutally. Hence, knowing and knowledge was a labor that very few in the society were bothered with.

It was when a small minority of people began a movement which ascribed darkness to ignorance and hence began the mega-movement to extract humans from the darkness of ignorance. While there is bliss in ignorance, this version of bliss is incomplete and inadequate. There was a small number of seekers who glorified the so-called real bliss but then also eschewed and humiliated the ignorant. Others even abused and exploited the ignorance based on the newly acquired power of knowledge. Knowing suddenly became important and it started getting equated with power.

KNOWLEDGE IS POWER

Because maybe only a few possessed knowledge, they had an edge and could use it wisely or misuse it. While there is some merit in knowledge is power, what type of knowledge and what type of power, is something I am doubtful of. This knowing is a very utilitarian knowing for a large number of people.

What is the utility of the knowledge, became the major focus. This also gave birth to the commercialization of the everyday exchange of information into the mega-enterprise of News media. Those who would know the arrival and departure details of a vessel would stand to benefit financially. Hence began the proliferation of knowing information accurately and prior to others knowing them.

However, in this era knowing had two aspects to it. The first was access and the second was remembering. Since access was either limited or interrupted, remembering whatever knowledge was acquired was equally paramount. But then came in the devices that lit fire in the underbelly of knowing, which is remembering. Devices and internet made knowledge accessible and uninterruptedly available to everyone. If something is available to everyone, then it is no more a competitive edge. So, the race began to acquire and disseminate knowledge rapidly. So much comes to us every day and when everything is important, then whether you like it or not important also becomes normal. Moreover, due to the easy availability of information upon demand, remembering became obsolete.

REMEMBERING IS OBSOLETE

This is also referred to as cognitive atrophy where due to the introduction of a given technology, humans give up on one of their acquired or real ability. The ability to remember routes and phone numbers is on the brink of extinction. The need to remember birthdays and anniversaries is gone because Facebook and LinkedIn will remind you every day. The need to remember techniques to do fast calculations is obsolete because calculators are quicker and unbelievably accurate at it. It was so amazing to not have to remember so many necessary and unnecessary things. But at the same time, with the information overload a new type of cognitive skill became necessary and that is retrieval.

RETRIEVAL IS THE KEY

Retrieval of information quickly became important because otherwise you are always looking for a needle in the haystack. Without proper retrieval mechanism, the advances made through technology were lost due to the time wasted in finding and retrieving the needed information. It was becoming a zero-sum game. Depending on when an individual is born, they would have had to make peace with applying their brain and cognitive faculties in a certain way either for knowing, remembering or for retrieving.

The three epochs of education and learning are knowledge is power, remembering is obsolete, and retrieval is the key are the epochs of partial dependence. Now we have the onslaught of large language models powered by machine learning and other sophisticated artificial intelligence. While premature now, they will learn superfast. Their ability to work on their weaknesses is astronomical and immediate. Soon the epoch of more or less complete dependence will begin.

IGNORANCE IS ONCE AGAIN A BLISS

Dependence on technology and gadgets will foster a different shade of ignorance resulting in a bliss. How long will this dependence-based ignorance and subsequent bliss will last is yet to be seen. But very soon questions such as why I need to waste time in educating myself will start arising and rightly so because the answers with the possibilities of it happening is not too far from horizon. Kids will be heard saying that just incorporate a chip in my brain and keep updating software for different skills. Very similar to what we have seen in the matrix movie, where they say things, such as download helicopter pilot skills, and the person in the matrix has the skills required to navigate one of the most complex and advanced helicopters. Elon Musk's company has successfully demonstrated the incorporation of a programmable chip in the brain. In MIT and in other labs, research on nanobots to directly support and manage your brain is underway. What will the system of education look and feel like in such epoch of bliss.

There will be the back-end side that will constantly be involved in developing program files that can be downloaded. Program files for swimming, accountancy, CPR, dancing the tango, filing taxes, performing medical procedure, and more will be developed and become available. There is a front-end website where one logs in and chooses skills and downloads the program. These programs can be on subscription model, or a limited time offer or a lifetime basis with full servicing including debugging and updating. Hence the bliss in a different shade of ignorance will prevail.

A CHALLENGED PERSPECTIVE ON STREAMLINING OF EDUCATION

The history of education is the history of learning. Learning initially and mainly through mimicking. Our learning begins when we start mimicking our parents. Children learn from observing their parents more than by listening to everything their parents tell them. So, some learning happens naturally. This often comes even before a parent comes into the picture. This learning is the beginning of learning about the self. But this self is the most basic self, mostly concerned with survival. Survival requires nourishment, security, and pro-creation. At the very initial stage, the only thing that a just-born baby is concerned about among the three is nourishment. It needs to learn to know when it is hungry and what it needs to due to acquire its mother's attention. Much later comes the part of assisted learning. A parent holds on to the hand of a youngling to ensure that it can keep its balance. Once it is able to then the parent slowly stops holding the hand.

Learning about the cursory self, learning about the use of our organs on which we have voluntary control, learning about things that help us survive and sustain. Later on, we developed the aspects of learning about better and realized living. Among our ancestors, acquiring food and water were of utmost significance and hence all majority of learning and mostly mimicking based learning revolved around the acquisition of food and water. Preparation and storage were secondary traits that needed to be developed. Somewhere somehow compartmentalization in the roles came into being here where the ones that went out engaged in acquisition and the ones that remained back engaged in preparation and storage. I strongly feel that excess and abundance brought in the need to organize and civilize. Learning to survive required acquiring and storing food or learning to snatch food acquired and stored by others. Once the basics were taken care of then the attention shifted to what the real purpose of education and learning should be.

Imparting learnings to enhance the quality of life and thought has for as long as we know followed a similar route; from the more experienced and learned to the less experienced and learned. The singular movement and flow of knowledge and wisdom has been as constant as the river always coming down from a mountain and flowing ultimately to the ocean and not the other way around.

Suppose now due to pseudo-heightened realization, one may argue that an ocean does not need any more water. It is already full and unlimited. Adding more water to the ocean is not going to make any difference to the ocean. Similarly, a human is the ocean, and ensuring that multiple rivers of knowl-edge flow toward him or her or they/them is pointless. This is the point of conflict. Most humans don't ever realize that they are oceans. They keep living miserable and unfulfilled lives thinking that they are some ponds that rely on rivers and rains or some underground source to keep them filled. To eliminate this ignorance a teacher with more experience and knowledge is warranted.

While learning can happen anytime anywhere, mostly it happens between individuals that are visibly belonging to different generations. A teacher having traveled though the rough road of life and having gone through the challenges is in a much better position to guide students of a different generation to get where he or she or they have somehow managed to successfully reach. For a large portion of humanity this destination is heaven or its equivalent in one form or the other. Teachers show the way to this destination and students follow. But what happens if the student chooses a different destination which the teacher has not yet traveled or arrived at. This is when the distinction between a teacher and a student is diminished. This is when they both either become co-travelers or they part ways as their destinations don't match. A traditional guru or a modern teacher cannot teach you to build an empire like Amazon or Google or Microsoft. Sadly, the founders of these companies can also not teach with conviction the things that the next generation of humans can due to build an empire like theirs. This is an unfortunate form of poverty that we are faced with in the 21st century.

In the earlier times, there was a consensus about the final destination of life. Moksha or enlightenment, release from sufferings and salvation was the destination. No matter what an individual did, it was all a means to achieve this goal of salvation. This consensus allowed for a system of education to prevail. This consensus allowed for the development and cementing of the roles of the major actors in the system of education. This consensus allowed for mutual respect between the different means, forms, methods, ideologies, and actions in the system of education because they were all exploring and examining ways to get to the same destination. The different means, forms, methods, ideologies, and actions evolved with the realization that humans have a varying degree of strengths and weaknesses. So based on the strength and weakness of each individual, he or she or they were able to adopt a given means to reach the final destination.

In the 21st century, I am, and we all are observing the outcomes of a serious mutation in the system of education. A general waywardness is rampant where the means, forms, methods, ideologies, and actions are misperceived as the destinations. The absence of singularity or in other words the absence of consensus pertaining to the destination is proving to be greatly detrimental. The singular consensus has been replaced by multiple micro-consensus channeling all learning and human efforts toward the means, forms, methods, ideologies, and actions, and nothing beyond.

TECHNOLOGY: THE BIG GENERATIONAL DIFFERENTIATOR

TEHCNOLOGY has changed the face of education in the 21st century. I will keep this section relatively brief because if elaborated too much it can become a book in itself. So, I will identify key issues and the rest you, my dear reader, are already living it. Let me begin by raising a question that will help frame the topic.

What is the impact of internet on learning is where I would like to begin. Internet has made all previous immobile repositories of knowledge greatly redundant. Let me explain this with an example. Outside of the classrooms, globally, one of the best sources of knowledge and information were these incredible things called Encyclopedia. At its peak, they were sold alphabetically. There would be a massive hard bound book which gave you myriad of useful information for everything that say for example started with letter "U". An Encyclopedia set would be one of the most prized possessions for countless families. What happened to Encyclopedias? Encyclopedia has pretty much become a word that pops up at times in advanced spelling bee competitions. Other than that Encyclopedia, the word, and Encyclopedia, the world class repositories of knowledge are both highly endangered and almost extinct species.

So, what has replaced Encyclopedia? You want to take any guesses. Encyclopedias which were researched written and compiled by experts is replaced by a volunteer run internet-based repository called Wikipedia. Wikipedia is the largest educator of our times with unimaginable reach. Technology and generations have a layered relationship. While the elderly people were thought of as guardians and sentinels of knowledge and information, here we see that an organization mainly run by young people is now the guardian and sentinel of all human knowledge and information. In earlier times, people used to be suspicious about something if it was not included in Encyclopedia. Now if something does not show up on Wikipedia, a question could be raised about its existence. Such has become our nature of dependence on it.

This is just the tip of the iceberg. Educational environments, pedagogies, curricula, assessments, and much more is highly dependent on technology. At my university, we use a learning management system (LMS). I often like to throw students a curved ball and give them assignments in class that are not on the learning management system, which they have to submit in the next class. Invariably atleast 40% of the students will not have done the work. And their immediate go to argument will be that but the system did not give us due date, or it was not there on the system. This indicates to me is that what happens in the class in front of them does not matter to them unless it is on the system. This is similar to the funny notion that unless you make it Facebook official you are not engaged or in a relationship.

Also, it is not easy to keep up with the pace of technology. So many changes and so much is offered as technological affordances that it is hard to keep up. In universities these days it is very hard to come by any faculty who does not use an LMS. During the pandemic, suddenly I found myself teaching not just to my student but also to her cat, his uncle, her boyfriend, and even to a favorite soft toy. Personally, I loved it. But I get that many others were frustrated with it. No eye contact, delayed response, seeing so many personal spaces, and in general lack of control can be frustrating both for the student and the teacher. The cohort of students that I see now in college don't know how to learn or hold themselves to rigor. The well documented learning loss during the remote era of pandemic has cut deeply. Technology enabled us to go on. In many instances, technology has buffered the negative impacts of remote schooling and learning, and even yielded superior outcomes.[4] However, often times I think that it may not have been so bad to pause. What was the obsessive need to keep going in a time of crisis. Not being able to pause and keep going on is also I feel a generational thing. Nonetheless, I feel that the pandemic-based infusion of technology has loosened the elastic and once it is loosened then it cannot be tightened again. So, with this knowledge and sensitivity, we have to move forward with generational synergy.

The value of technologically being savvy is disproportional in the market food-chain. If you can code or work with AI, then your demand and value in the market is very high in contrast to someone who can tell you everything that there is to know about the uniforms during the Civil war. I have already indicated that I want to keep this section brief as its a slippery slope. I want to end this section by noting that despite the influx of technology and it not going away anywhere, kids in America in a Gallup poll have rated schools at an unfortunate B- in terms of how they are doing. While we are infusing more and more technology, we have to also be mindful of the diminishing marginal utility of it and if its benefits have plateaued then we must pause and rethink about what is needed to do better.

CONCLUSION

I want to conclude this chapter by identifying a bigger issue that pans across generations. As far as education is concerned, everyone involved in it is burning out at a rate faster than any other professional activity. An approximate average of 4 out of 10 K-12 teachers and university professors are "always" feeling burned out.[5] This is higher than employees of every other industry. Students are not happy. Neither are teachers happy. If both are burning out, then who is benefitting from this entire enterprise? Not to forget that amidst all, the lesbian gay and bisexual Gen Zers are suffering from mental health issues the most in comparison to other groups.[6]

Generationally, issues of physical safety were never something that kids or teachers had to be much concerned about. But now with the consistent slew of mass shootings these worries, and tensions are playing at the back of mind of students and teachers. Another issues that individuals who are connected with education are facing is that teachers are being paid less and students are paying more fees. Both are being strained. In this tug-of-war, no one is due to emerge as a winner. Moreover, the social respect and status of a teacher is also watering down.

I am 40 years old, and my undergraduate students are between 18 and 22 years. An average 20 years of age difference seems to make huge difference as far as our mindsets, thought processes, attitude toward life, and more are concerned. It blows my mind. We both speak English, but I am not exaggerating when I say that we both speak different languages. I cannot speak their language and they cannot speak mine. So often times we find ourselves as the captains of ships waving at one another while passing each other in the middle of the night. Could generations sharing a longer life together be an issue? Absolutely it would be, but it can be avoided through cultivating intergenerational harmony. It is therefore Mariano Sanchez and Matthew Kaplan suggest that multigenerational classrooms bring with them the potential to "learn about other generational groups and positions that are tacitly or explicitly present in the classroom... and to entertain new possibilities for intergenerational interaction and cooperation."[7]

The European Network for Intergenerational Learning (ENIL) defines intergenerational learning as a partnership based on reciprocity and mutuality involving people of different ages in gaining skills, values, and knowledge. The benefits of intergenerational classrooms are that we can uncover myriad generational positions, experiment and identify apt spaces for facilitating better generational interaction and communication. Many aspects of design might be needed to develop a learning space that can accommodate the tacit and explicit generational needs. Different generations have different learning priorities and approach learning spaces accordingly so knowing these would be beneficial. There is one course about mass media and society that I teach to freshman students. A few times I have had a non-traditional student in the course from military or industry. It was visibly clear that their generational priorities are so different and while it is easy to ignore them as a minority, it is difficult but important to include them and create an optimal space for learning. Harnessing generational synergy will improve the intergenerational understanding contributing more to the overall harmony. The main objective here would be to nullify the intergenerational ambivalence as much as possible.

NOTES

1.   https://www.ncbi.nlm.nih.gov/pmc/articles/PMC8913502/
2.   Avery, C., & Turner, S. (2012). Student loans: Do college students borrow too much–or not enough? *Journal of Economic Perspectives*, 26, 165–192. https://doi.org/10.1257/jep.26.1.165
3.   Sánchez, M., & Kaplan, M. (2014). Intergenerational learning in higher education: Making the case for multigenerational classrooms. *Educational Gerontology*, 40(7), 473–485. https://doi.org/10.1080/03601277.2013.844039
4.   https://news.gallup.com/opinion/gallup/388502/better-technology-produced-better-learning-outcomes-during-pandemic.aspx
5.   https://news.gallup.com/opinion/gallup/400670/putting-teacher-burnout.aspx
6.   https://news.gallup.com/opinion/gallup/507881/lgb-gen-members-anxious-stressed-peers.aspx
7.   Hagedorn-Hatfield, R. L., Hood, L. B., & Hege, A. (2022, February). A decade of college student hunger: What we know and where we need to go. *Front Public Health*, 25(10), 837724. https://doi.org/10.3389/fpubh.2022.837724. PMID: 35284399; PMCID: PMC8913502.

4

BUSINESS

Businesses, worldwide, have been impacted adversely by the inability to manage linear and non-linear Multigenerationality. This inability results in subpar corporate performance and delay in achievement of organizational goals. Different generations have different outlooks and approaches on how to conduct business and achieve business goals. The preference of a member from a given generation to do business in a certain way is typically the problem. But neither the remedy to this issue nor the malady is simple. Consumers and ecology are on the short end of the stick here.

Frictions, in general, and tensions emerge from intergenerational disharmony in business and corporate settings. They often take the forms of disagreements and discord, hostile work environment, suppression of ideas and the people behind the ideas, toxic work culture, and more. before the introduction of technology and disruptions fueled by it, corporations only suffered from the crisis of linear Multigenerationality. In linear Multigenerationality, superior and subordinate are in the descending order of ages with the superior being older and the subordinate being younger. Earlier, it was hard to imagine a 25-year-old being the boss of a 55-year-old corporate veteran. But in the age of technological disruption, this is also a reality. And we are not yet fully equipped to deal with this level of non-linear multigenerationality where the descending order of ages has gone for a toss. Family run businesses are seeing tremendous friction too. Kids don't want to do the same business as their father precisely because they want to avoid conflicts and develop their own identity. Younger generation believes that identities can be developed only if you create your own brand and your own business. A strong evolving trend is to see your father not as a source of learning and training but as an individual who does not want you to flourish so keeps controlling you and dismissing your ideas. While this argument does have some merit, it is not entirely true. I will discuss this in more detail later in the chapter where I talk about the intergeneration insensitivity.

I came across an instance, which may elucidate the complexity and the perplexity of the absence of intergenerational harmony. The instance is about a father and a daughter. I came across this case while traveling overseas. Multigenerationality was not dealt with reasonably and the result was that the daughter quit. In this case I am not going to paraphrase or give you my understanding and summary of it. I am sharing what was shared with me verbatim and then through an email. Read the below and then we will discuss things further.

CASE OF INTERGENERATIONAL DISHARMONY IN FAMILY BUSINESS

After spending two and a half years in a multinational corporation, researching the successes and failures of various brands, understanding consumer reactions to marketing campaigns, and recognizing the significance of purposeful branding, I decided to join my father's business. My father, a self-made entrepreneur who initiated his venture at the age of 16, had built a thriving hospitality business catering to top hotels in India. With an MBA and work experience under my belt, I believed we could propel the business to new heights.

In the initial weeks, I closely observed my father, engaging with everyone in the office and relishing every aspect of the business. Our time together, attending meetings, negotiating deals, and sharing meals, was particularly enjoyable. I admired him both as a businessman and a person.

As time progressed, I recognized the need for the business to establish an online presence. Taking the initiative, I ventured into website development, logo designing, and managing our social media platforms. Working in my own area allowed me to contribute meaningfully without encroaching on my father's space. Maybe deep down, I knew, that if we worked together on certain things, there would be many differences of opinion, and I did not want to rock the boat.

However, I soon realized that working in silos was not sustainable for our business. I began expressing my opinions on various aspects of the business, from bookkeeping and sales to hiring and overall development. Personally, I found my father's practices to be somewhat old-fashioned, particularly his tendency to micromanage even when dedicated staff was in place. This led to disagreements, with him often dismissing my perspective.

The blending of familial and business roles became apparent, especially when my father exhibited an overprotective nature. Despite my comfort in business scenarios, he resisted letting me attend meetings alone in male-dominated environments. This tension extended beyond the office, affecting our family dynamics. To avoid conflict at the dinner table, I adjusted my mealtime and withdrew into my own space at home.

The frustration and agony reached a breaking point, prompting me to question my decision to join the family business. Yearning for peace, harmony, and a return to my happy family, I contemplated leaving and returning to my previous job. Feeling like a caged bird, I eventually made the difficult decision to quit and pursue my dream of obtaining a PhD. Now, after four years, I am immersed in my research, content with my decision, and my relationship with my father has returned to normal. Sometimes, you need to see the larger picture in life and act accordingly for the greater good.

The above case should give you an insight into the complexity of the issue and the different ways in which adjustments and compromises are to be made. Now there is one thing to keep in mind here, and that is that this is the story from only one side. This is the daughter's story in the words of the daughter. It is her perspective. So, it might even look like the older generation is the one that doesn't understand and is the real villain. And while that might be true, let's say for argument's sake in this case, it is most certainly not true in all cases. So, I caution you against arriving to a conclusion where one generation is exclusively the culprit and the other a victim because that is certainly not true. Every generation, whether older or younger, is equally ignorant and insensitive, and intentionally or unintentionally controls and hurts the other generation and in that process also hurting business.

After interacting with countless such young and old businesspersons, I noticed that the disagreements and disharmony was mostly present in the styles and approaches rather than the more serious ideological, ethical, and other important aspects. The absence of respect of the younger businesspersons toward the approach of their elders is a bit demeaning and counterproductive. The younger generations that are entering the family business often suffer from the savior syndrome. They feel that they will come and their way of doing things will propel the business to new heights. However, they don't often see the larger picture and in my humble opinion 9 out of 10 times focus on giving the company simply a cosmetic makes over. This cosmetic makeover comes in the form of vision, mission, logo, strategic goal, website, and social media presence. They rely on technology and standardized systems more than humans. This is not how their parents and elders in the business see things. Moreover, not every business can become the posterchild for internet and social media coming in to save the day.

Parents, at the same time, feel that they are giving their child a sandbox to play in when they let them play and fool around with logos and vision and mission statements. They know deep down that none of this makes much of a difference to the business. So instead of engaging them in aspects that can show significant results on the bottom-line, they let them play with things that add cost to the company with limited return and impact on profitability. The older generation is also so rooted in the way they have done business that no matter how poor their management of the business is, they continue to take pride in the fact that they have somehow survived and succeeded.

A big reason for generational conflicts between generations is the big difference in the long-term goals of the generations. Most members of the older generations don't wish or intend to grow their business beyond a certain scale. Yes, this is true. If you exclude the handful large businesses, a very large proportion of businessmen don't have tremendously big aspirations. After having spent atleast 2 decades in the business/entrepreneurial world, members of the older generations have reached their saturation and have resorted exclusively to the goal of sustaining the business. Whereas the new blood wants nothing short of the moon. The difference between such fundamental attitudes makes the member of the younger generation like a woodpecker constantly hammering on the older generation to grow and be big and dominate the market. This does nothing other than contributing to the increment in the nuisance value of the younger generations. The woodpeckers, on the other hand feel that the older generation do not care for their aspirations.

In tandem with generational attitudes and aspirations comes along the issues of trust and performance. Just to be clear, trust and performance have an intricate relationship. If they were on social media their relationship status would be complicated (for those who know this understand it, for those who don't know, don't try). There is no trust without performance, and at the same time there is no performance without trust. Now this binary creates a vacuum, where neither can thrive. Younger generation wants trust so that they can perform. The older generation argues that how do we trust you without seeing your performance. With no prior performance, how can I invest much of what I have earned in the past 2 decades. If I do so. I would be labeled as foolish. This catch 22 situation is very damaging when one seeks to establish Intergenerational Harmony.

The same is seen in well-established corporates in a slightly different fashion. After carefully observing this phenomenon in the corporate and start-up world, I concluded that the notion of generation plays out differently in this setting. It has very little to do with your physical age. Generations here are created and defined based on proximity. See Fig. 4 below.

Generation is a dynamic concept. Generations are not to be looked at exclusively from an age point of view, especially in the business world. Generational hierarchy (see Fig. 4) helps you look at generations differently and in the process understand them better in a large corporate setting. Generation in this case is understood based on the proximity to the founder of the company. Every idea, every start-up, every innovation, every corporation has a founder or founders. There will always be a very small group of people who have directly worked with the founder. They were part of the small team that was initially brought in when the idea started becoming big. These individuals are the second generation in a corporate setting. They have affinity for the founder and a unique sense of loyalty to the vision of the founder. Regardless of how relevant or anachronistic the vision could be, the second generation sticks with it. They become the custodians of the vision and ways of the founder. They are the keepers of the stories. They also become the repositories or the experts on the founders and the founders' way of running the company. Often since they became part of the company when it was small with limited budgets their mindset still continues to be the one which does not necessarily approve of many things, for example celebrations to motivate employees. This is mainly because when they were starting, they were self-motivated and did not require or even if they required were not granted such opportunities. Being small everyone knew everyone and about their lives intimately. They have much more of a family vibe than a team vibe.

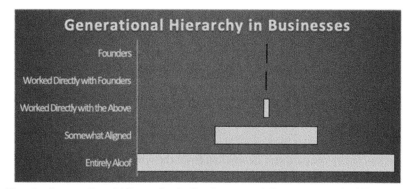

Fig. 4. Generational Hierarchy in Business and Entrepreneurial World.

In the third generation, I observed those individuals who have worked directly with the second generation and not the founders. The founders or the first generation is a very small group to begin with and often as companies grow, they become inaccessible very quickly. They are more accessible through their public appearances, news and social media but not in the office. A limited number of the third generation would have some random contact whatsoever with the first generation. The members of the third generation are the promoters of the stories. They take pride in who they have listened the story from. In other words, how close the person, they heard the stories from, was to the founders. They are the last generation who possess excitement simply out of loyalty and proximity. These are also the makers and breakers of the company ethos. While there might be a generally positive outlook about the founder's vision and way of running the business, it is from here that things start changing. Anachronisms are identified but not necessarily acted upon due to the proximity to the custodians or the second generation. This generation does increase the status of the first generation, the founders, to the those who are larger than life. As promoters of stories they accentuate, embellish, exaggerate the stories, the vision, and the way of life. And take it to a large group of unconnected folks. This group of unconnected folks are the fourth generation. The size of the membership in this one is substantially larger than the prior three.

The fourth generation is, depending on your perspective and ideological positioning, the one that either brings about the evolution of the vision and way of life or mutates it. Due to the large number of people included in this generation, the focus starts shifting from what I can do for the vision of the founder to what the vision of the founder can do for me. Hence, this is the generation with somewhat alignment to the founder's vision. You may have inferred thus far, that the second, third, and fourth generations present a diminishing trend in allegiance to the vision and ways of life of the founder. The fourth generation is pretty much the last generation that shows any care or consideration for a certain way of life and vision. This is where the link breaks. The fifth generation, which is largest in number, are the ones that are far removed and are entirely self-absorbed.

When the members of the fifth generation join an organization, they are introduced and exposed to the vision of the founder for anywhere between 5 and 15 minutes during the orientation that a member of the fourth generation gives. The fifth generation are, once again depending on your ideological position, either the parasites benefitting from the work and sacrifice of the first three generations or those ignorant fools who for a few peanuts keep dancing to the tunes of the unknown music conductor. As a cumulative, this generation is important as a group, but individually, they hold no significance. They are dispensable. Moreover, they are also due to their own lack of interest or as a design kept aloof about the larger picture. They are disconnected and disjointed. They are invited into the culture on a need only basis and are also uninvited when the need ends.

These are the five generations that I was able to distinguish and discern as living and co-existing within organizations these days. And it is between these generations that there is a lack of harmony. This is much truer of the start-up and entrepreneurial world. Using age for understanding the macro divisions is not the most apt given the emergence of technologically inspired disruptions in the development and progress of businesses. I realized this during my study because I was not able to accurately decipher the absence of harmony when I tried to utilize age as the lens for understanding generations. It was only after I applied proximity to the founder when the many prevalent discords started becoming clear. The major area of conflict comes from the fact that the founder did some things his or her or their way ignoring the norms and policy for which they are hailed as revolutionaries and disrupters and risktakers. But those very same things that led to the initial and subsequent success are now prohibited from trying and implementing due to policies and norms. Here what happens is that instead of the founders' vision and way of life, policies of the organization become the driving force. The more you are removed further, the lesser your entitlement becomes when it comes to forgiveness. In the fourth and fifth generation there is almost no concept of forgiveness for such "deviant" behaviors.

Now it is not that the situation of synergy is dire, because there are project-based cooperation and joint actions that occur. But what is missing is the harmony. From the point of view of trust and respect the situation becomes stressed. Between the second and the fifth generation this is a big issue. The fifth generation does not have much respect for the second generation because they think that this group of people have lived their entire lives colonized by the vison of another person. Such lack of respect unfortunately fosters distance. From the individuals of the second generations' point of view, they cannot trust members of the fifth generation because they are not at all aligned or are in any proximity of founder's vision. When there is absence of trust, caution is exercised in involving an individual in major decision-making process. This prevents colleagues from coming together as a harmonious whole. In the next section, I offer some insights on how to repair this.

WHAT CAN YOU DO IF YOU ARE A CORPORATE?

Due to intergenerational disharmony, businesses lose out on a chunk of their efficiency and profitability. And the sad part is that fixing this is easy. There is not a huge investment required to fix some of these issues of disharmony. If you are part of a business or a corporate, and are struggling from such issues, then I offer to you 3 possible things to try out for resolving such differences and bringing in more harmony.

(1) *Corporation versus cult*: the first and foremost thing that needs to happen for enhancing intergenerational harmony is that if you have to realize that you are in a corporation/business environment and not a cult. The issues begins when despite being in a corporation the expectations are that of a cult. The dynamics of respect and trust are very different in a cult. The very nature of a cult does not allow for greater deviation and hence it might take multiple decades or even centuries and countless generations to start seeing the issues of respect and trust.

One has to be mindful that in a corporation there is never the absolute surrender kind of phenomenon as seen in cults. Also, the entire aspect of offering monetary remuneration in exchange of expertise or services is at the core of the two individuals coming together in a corporation. Nobody is ever paid for their allegiance toward the vision with no offering of services or expertise. The clarity of the distinction between a corporation and cult, and the basics driving both is helpful in working on Empathy for a member of a different generation. It is only through empathy that we can develop healthy thresholds to work with someone despite some differences, and to cultivate trust and respect about one another.

(2) *Respect*: building respect between the generations should be a high priority for any organization. Generational entitlement is the key to building and curating respect in an organization with relative ease. Generational entitlement based on proximity or technological superiority is the culprit. Any kind of superiority complex or inferiority complex contributes to entitlement. Stripping of generational entitlement is necessary because it brings everyone on a level playing field. In that level playing field, respect is organic and not due to some artificially created hierarchy. It may sound counter-intuitive, but hierarchy is detrimental to respect, because hierarchy typically is skewed toward linear respect. To address the issue of respect here are some quick ways.

Team exercises focusing on the significance of the existence of a human and not his or her or their ability and achievement are a good starting point. Ingraining the need to value your colleague just because he or she or they are and not what they do through a story sharing and a consequent conversation about it is a good start. This can be done also by the organization where they through emails or posters celebrate the helpful stories outside of work of a given person. Knowing a person outside of their abilities and achievements, and more through their kindness is a subtle way to inspire respect. In the corporate world, respect that emerges from ability and achievements is conditional respect and therefore is fragile whereas, the respect that emerges from knowing the kind and altruistic side of a person is more long-term. Through this corporations can inspire respect among colleagues of different generation.

(3) *Trust*: lack of respect for others generates an apathy toward the other and also leads to a negative spiral of thinking, where the ethos of a member of other generation is challenged. This impacts trust between generations negatively. To develop the ability to put trust in a member of another generation one must be clear about what the other person can give and take. For example, a member of the fifth generation can only give expertise. His ability to offer lifelong loyalty at that level is highly limited. In such situations, the other person needs to be trusted with their expertise. Unconditional allegiance to the values of the founder right from the get-go is an unreal expectation. Unless you live those values and provide opportunities to take risks with assured forgiveness, no employee will want to take any risk which would rock the boat.

There is also a slightly different way of looking at generations aside from the proximity point of view. Although they are more of categories of individuals involved in different roles than generations but there is some merit in looking at them, so I present them to you in brief. These generations or classifications are of owners, partners, stakeholders, employees, and contractors. Contractors are often from the fifth generation. They by policy have an extremely less stake in the company. Employees are mostly found in the fourth generation. Somewhat allegiance but mostly restricted to the orientation and other HR gatherings. Partners and stakeholders are in alignment with the second and third generations who express higher alliance with the vision and goals. Founders are once again in the first generation. By using proximity and role, one can get a better understanding of the involvement and engagement of a particular individual.

CONCLUSION

Businesses and corporations exist to make profit. If they don't make profit sooner or later, they cease to exist. Efficiency is highly prized within such settings. If efficiency is not on your side, then it is working against you. This is what happened in the automobile industry when it initially started using robots and artificial intelligence in the assembly line. Despite the heavy investment in technology and collaboration with it in the assembly line processes, there was marginal increment seen in the production. On the contrary in many instances production reduced. Artificial Intelligence was not as sharp as it is today because of limited computing ability as well as less availability of data. It was very hard for AI powered robots to improvize. They would often get stuck. Having diverse teams is favorable and not cultivating IH is like investing in the AI of the 80s.

Multigenerational teams within corporates working and collaborating with one another is inevitable. Multiple types of multigenerational teams are what I see as the strong emerging trend of future in the entrepreneurial and corporate world. Corporation is an exceedingly competitive space and therefore you also see lot of burn out in such settings. Although in the chapter about education we have learned that teachers are the most burned-out workers of all. IH has a fundamental role to play in ensuring that the corporation is working at its peak efficiency because even if you have the expertise but then if the expertise does not get along well and is not put to good use, it is more of a liability than an asset. With IH there are three things that a business can excel at. IH enables nimbleness within an organization. IH breeds loyalty for one another and together for the company. And IH can go a long way in cultivating creativity within a business.

Nimbleness, loyalty, and creativity are three mission critical areas for any major corporation or business, especially in the agile era of the 21st century characterized by constant unprecedented chance. Imagine a major global bank that does trillions worth of transaction every year. The kind of cyber threats that a financial institution of this magnitude can experience in the 21st century is unthinkable. From the chairman of the bank to the person who cashes check has to have the above three. Every major threat brings about changes in the bank's modus operandi. It is the nimbleness of the employees that enables them to quickly switch to the new change and also in turn help their customers through that. Banking has changed more in the last 10 years than in the previous 100 years. Constant creativity along with technological superiority is required to develop new processes and protocols to safeguard the bank from cyber threats. And there is no need to stress the importance of loyalty in a banking environment. IH creates an environment where different generations can harness their own competitive advantages and pull everyone together. If IH exists many potentials can transform into actionable plausibility. Without IH, the resistance and internal conflicts will kill every change and every new idea, not because it does not have merit but because it comes from a member of different generation.

Going back to the realm of family business, if the father and daughter had got along well, the business would have most likely progressed with an integrated intergenerational effort. If there is IH no daughter or son will ever have to leave their family business to avoid conflict or to find their own identity in something else if there identity is preserved and projected in the family business. Business owners will have to learn the art of how to include their next generation in their family business otherwise we will see a sudden decline in a large number of businesses that are operating for decades and centuries. IH is a starting point and the end point for ensuring that the family business actually becomes a multigenerational family business where a family and its members come together to successfully run it.

5

FAMILY

Family is the premier and the only naturally occurring sector of human civilization. All the other sectors (Education, Religion, Corporation, Government) are artificially created by humans. The unit of family has been a cornerstone for organizing and evolving humanity into what it is today. The modern lifestyle and absence of generational synergy has resulted in a rupture in the bonding and structuring of the family. In my professional opinion this is the top most priority area for channeling efforts to enhance intergenerational harmony.

COVID-19 did the dual task of not only separating many people from one another by geopolitical restrictions on travel and quarantine but also united many willing and unwilling parties. COVID-19 managed the impossible of bringing families together outside of Thanksgiving and Christmas. Two to three generations living together and in some exceptional cases even four generations living together. This sort of intergenerational shared existence has not been seen in the western world. While generations and families living together is sort of rare in the western world, it is quite the norm in many eastern countries. The biggest of them all in terms of population is India. In India generations live together. This togetherness is the chief reason for the strong cultural transference of values and traditions.

The coming together of multiple generations in one home is going to see an increase in the coming years. There are several reasons for this shift. I will elaborate on some of those and will also provide my observations and a few speculations of what the new avatar of multigenerational living will be. Regardless, it is paramount to prepare ourselves and be ready for intergenerational harmony. The dynamics of access, voice, dependence, reverence, and hierarchy have changed tremendously in the last 30 years and the new multigenerational living is therefore, in my humble speculation, not able to provide the same warmth and comfort. The rough edges will lead to increased friction. But I am optimistic that within all the mega categories in which multigenerationality needs to be addressed family has the highest potential to turn around for good. I am also banking on the old saying that blood is thicker than water for this turn around. Let us look at the reasons for the expansion of multigenerational families.

TECHNOLOGY

Technology is a great enabler. It can make many things, otherwise unimaginable, happen. One such thing that technology is making happen is the work-from-home (WFH) revolution. If not for the real estate lobbies, WFH would already have been the norm. Technologies such as internet connectivity and high-speed computing are empowering many to overcome geographical restrictions. While this facility to work from anywhere gave rise to the subculture of digital nomadism, it has had a major impact on creating work from home culture. Who does not want to be in the proximity and vicinity of their loved ones. Families with kids, pets, and elder parents in need of care prefer this a lot. Applications such as ZOOM and google meet have brought families together as well as closer. The WFH has enabled countless to return home as the need to be in another city to make a living vanished with WFH.

Moreover, it also has brought families closer. Families that are geographically spread out now have regular meet and greet online. Many families are still holding their weekly zoom get togethers. Surprisingly or unsurprisingly, it is the older generation who has held on to this weekly gathering online. Most Gen Z and millennials have slowly and silently dropped out of this habit. They will pop in from time to time and then disappear. The technology enabled WFH culture has most certainly contributed positively to bringing members of family and generations together and this will only increase.

COST-EFFICIENCY

Looking deeply from a behavioral insights point of view, perceptions about the value of money have been influenced by the pandemic. Something that has been observed globally is revenge shopping. As soon as people were able to go out after the pandemic, they started splurging money on myriad of things.

However, what has been influenced the most is the value of saving money. A large number of decisions in the matters of high-involvement products and lifestyle choices are indicative of the trend where people want to save more. One such way of saving money was through moving in with your family. In most cases, the family homes had ample room and were underutilized. Millennials and some gen Zs have made the migration of returning to their parents' home. This has saved them a lot of rent money. Rent money especially in big cities and metros is egregious. In cities like NYC, LA, London, and Mumbai where a large number of people live on rent, those who are able to do WFH have moved back. With the many restrictions and risks in big cities, the willingness to make compromise of space and place that people were willing to make has reduced. They don't mind going to larger homes with higher hygiene and lesser risks and no crowds. The preference and facility of enjoying delicious home cooked meals is an added motivation.

The cost efficiency factor has positively contributed to members of family migrating back to their homes. Empty nesters are no more empty nesters. Some reverse migration has happened where millennials have resorted back to renting their spaces but there is still a residual population that has continued to survive in the same arrangement. Migration, which was inspired during the pandemic, but had cost efficiency in the foundation of it has increased multigenerational homes globally. Rent was not the only avenue to save money. Furniture, food, travel, and connectivity are some more avenues where people were able to save money and living together was cost effective.

END OF LIFE WISDOM

Decisions change drastically because priorities change drastically when one is faced with end-of-life situation. It is often seen that people become magnanimous and altruistic after surviving a major accident or a near death experience. The COVID-19 pandemic brought millions face to face with death. Very few people can claim to have not lost a friend or a member of family during the pandemic. Globally, a massive surge in the end-of-life wisdom was seen among people. People in the age range of 25–40 had realizations what one would otherwise realize at age 80. This has changed people's priorities. Family, which was a latent priority, became an active priority. This too contributed to the coming of generations together under one roof.

LONELINESS

Mental health crisis is strengthening its grip on the society. One of the contributors to the mental health crisis is loneliness. Loneliness has increased substantially among the younger as well as the older generations. To earn a better living or to earn a degree young adults move out. Despite being surrounded by thousands of people these youngsters are lonely in their university dorms. Friends are a rare commodity. Universities all across the states are spending millions of dollars to increase the average number of friends per person by one.

Parents are lonely because their kids have left and after a certain age it is difficult to make new friends or move away. Grandparents are lonely because they have so much to say but no one to listen. Their kids and their grandkids are busy building their own lives. And as much as possible when they do spend and give time, it is not enough. All this has led to loneliness and many related anxieties. With greater awareness about the loneliness issue, more and more people are choosing to live with their family when they are going through a mental health crisis. Family is supposed to be one of the strongest support systems that anyone has outside of the state and federal provided support systems.

While above are some of the reasons why we will see more and more multi-generational homes in the future. Medical care is also contributing to this by ensuring that people are living long. Although people don't marry early as they used to in the past, since they live longer, they see their grandchildren and great grandchildren. Globally we have succeeded in keeping very many infections and diseases away, this has not only increased longevity but also improved the overall quality of life. A multi-generational home can be a tremendous source of joy and delight. It can also be a strong reason for the continuation of rituals and traditions and even be the reason for the survival of a culture. With that said, it becomes pertinent that the intricacies and challenges pertaining to multi-generational homes are identified and resolved so that it does not become a source of melancholy. When members of different generations come together and live together, they also bring their preferences attitudes habits and lifestyles with them.

ISSUES OF MULTIGENERATIONAL LIVING

Multigenerational living comes with its own downsides. To increase Intergenerational Harmony, it is important to be well versed with the downsides so that they can be avoided, or a greater threshold of tolerance can be developed to better prepare for multigenerational living. There are very many nuances to multigenerational living, but I will cover in this chapter only a few major ones.

MEDIA CONSUMPTION

Consumption of media varies greatly among member of different generations. In a multi-generational family, grandparents consume media very differently from how other generations do. Parents will consume media differently and with more responsibility, and kids are still a mystery. I say mystery because no one knows when and how they are able to find time and means needed to access things that are not meant for them. So their industriousness and resourcefulness are still a mystery that we have not been able to successfully crack. Older generation still consumes synchronous media. Every day at a certain given time they will stop whatever they are doing and somehow manage to situate themselves in front of a television to watch their favorite show. This would ideally be something that they have done for the last two decades. The have a loyalty to the concept and in many cases even to the presenter or the protagonist of the show.

The Gen. Xers and early millennials are the ones who still have synchronous connection but are also moving strongly toward the asynchronous world of streaming. It would not be entirely true to say that they are the ones who make the most of these services but since they have the money to pay for it, they are subscribers to these services. It is their children who are utilizing the asynchronous streaming services to the fullest. They don't stop whatever they are doing, instead make the algorithm of the streaming service remember how much they have seen of the show and will continue from there when they return to it. For the younger generations a large majority of viewing happens online and that too through their cell phone device. They choose the personal touch with their device over the communal TV watching.

Now what I'm going to say next is something that may be anecdotal, but I am sure that you will be able to relate to it. I have a niece who wants to watch shows that are about anime cartoons. I have another nephew who wants to exclusively watch content pertaining to nature and ecology. I have another nephew who likes to sing and therefore keeps listening to all the different tutorials on how to sing better. Now they choose to consume all of this on their cell phone. It also makes sense because not everyone in the family is going to enjoy anime cartoons or watching singing tutorials or looking at mountains or animals or birds all the time. What I have noticed is that if someone tries to show you something and you don't fall completely gaga over it, they will never show you anything else. So, you either have to fake enthusiasm or risk the person not engaging with you in this manner in the future. This kind of sensitivity and overreaction is especially common among Gen. Z's and some millennials.

Gen Z and millennials, in addition to being consumers are also producers of content. The actively produce and upload content on different streaming and social platforms that can be viewed by a large audience. This is another trait which is much more prevalent in the younger generations. This is also the group which spends a large amount of time percentage wise in consuming, producing, and streaming activities. Media occupies a lot of time share for these generation. It is important to understand all this because despite living in the same home, members of different generations are not able to come together always. There are very few shows or online content that all members of the family can enjoy together. All the streaming content that is very popular in most places is very difficult to watch with your family. The use of abusive language, promiscuous lifestyle, overindulgence and abuse of drugs and alcohol, and sexually explicit materials in the content dissuades the family from watching and enjoying together.

It is very safe to take your parents and grandparents for watching a movie in a movie theater in India. The censor board does whatever it does and ensures that anything that can create discomfort is well edited out of the movie. But the same movie can produce an entirely different experience when watched in a different country which has different censorship norms. A relative of mine recently told me that he went through a tremendously uncomfortable situation when he took his father-in-law to watch the recently released movie about the scientist Robert Oppenheimer. While the movie was exceptional and might even go on to win a lot of awards as well, the nudity shown in the movie made the experience very sour for his father-in-law as well as him. The same thing that made the viewing experience awkward would have most certainly been censored and edited out of the movie in a different culture. Censoring is both bad and good.

Media can be a great divider in the house. I say this because of what a student shared with me recently in the class. I have shared this earlier but I want to reiterate this from the perspective of media. My student told me that her family has not celebrated Thanksgiving or Christmas since the time of a certain presidential election. She said that her family is divided into two parts where one is an absolute fan, and the other side hates the gut of the person. She said that it has become impossible to get the entire family together because the keep arguing and debating over the different issues pertaining to the nation and it's well-being. They keep quoting from the news on social media and keep bickering about it. It has been well established that social media was weaponized to polarize people in the US and many other parts of the world. The society is already polarized but when polarization enters in a home, multigenerational living becomes challenging. The political polarizing is in a way no different than the division and polarization that young American display by choosing team Edward and team Jacob or even between fans of Taylor Swift and fans of Selena Gomez and fans of Justin Bieber. While polarization was the same, its implications were not as severe.

FOOD HABITS

This is a big one. Food brings people together. Food is the bonding agent amidst families and even cultures. Food is an area where the power dynamics are the most intricate and nuanced. Let us understand the complexities that food can introduce in a multigenerational family. One unsaid family tradition that transcended generational boundaries was the daily act of having meals together. The regularity and routinization of family meals, if not twice then for sure once a day, kept families together. The myriad of things that are shared and conversed during the mealtime kept family alive as a unit.

For as long as I can remember, mealtimes in our home are fixed and no matter where you are or what you might be doing, you abandon it all and make yourselves available at those times for eating lunch and dinner with the family. Our mealtimes were lunch between 12:30 and 1:00 p.m. in the afternoon and dinner at 8:30 p.m. in the evening. Even the times for tea and snacks in the early morning and early afternoon are fixed. However, since I don't drink tea those don't apply to me usually, but if I want something else during that time then I do need to be there.

There has always been regularization and routinization about cooking and consuming food. You are shamed for consuming it outside of those designated times. A very important observation about today's multigenerational family members living more like roommates than as a family was made by Professor Jagdish Sheth. Roommates share a home or an apartment but continue to live their independent existence in their rooms. Roommates come and go at a time of their choosing. There is neither any regulation nor any overlaps in the routines of roommates. On the contrary, an effort is often made to ensure reduction in such overlaps with the noble goal of not intruding one another's space. Despite having four roommates sharing a home, you are still alone in your room. You also for the most part confine yourself in your room and avoid hanging out in common areas. To avoid coming out to the kitchen many also purchase mini-refrigerator and microwave and keep some of the essential food items in their room. This further reduces the need to come into a common area. Families too are becoming like this.

COVID-19 has managed to keep everyone inside the house but has also unintentionally succeeded in keeping everyone apart in the house. I often visit my cousin who lives in the US. She has a loving family of seven. She and her husband have three kids. In addition, they have a dog. My cousin's father and my brother-in-law's mother also live in the same house. Three generations live in the same home. To me this is a matter of deep joy and pride that three generations are living together in the same household. But there are also certain things I have noticed, which are not exclusive to this home, but are an indication of the larger trend in multigenerational homes. It is observed everywhere. Due to the varying class timings and work meeting times, lunch time extents from noon to 2:30 p.m. Different members of the family come at different times, eat their lunch and go back. Sometimes they come, take the food, and go away. So, despite the prolonging of the lunch hour, the togetherness is substantially reduced.

The grandparents wake up early around 5 a.m. and go to sleep by 9:00 or 9:30 p.m. The kids wake up depending on when they are required to wake up and go to bed at an unknown time. The sandwich generation works hard to be the catalyst and adhere to the old regime, while allowing sufficient space to the newer lot to discover themselves in relative freedom. It's a tough balancing act, and I have always admired my cousin and her husband for doing this with utmost grace, patience, and care. I do see somewhat apathy or a lack of consideration in the Gen Z when it comes to food. Despite so much knowledge and focus on nutrition, their food habits are deeply problematic because they are restricted, erratic, and based on convenience. This often becomes a point of contention and conflict between generations in multigenerational homes.

Online food ordering and delivery services are not helping a whole lot. They are providing an option to an entire generation, which was not present for other generations. The presence of multiple cuisines on a dining table is quite common now. Parents eating staple regional food, daughter eating sushi, her siblings eating pizza would be incomprehensible some years ago. If I decided to not eat the food cooked by my mother, then I had no other option but to go to bed hungry. However, now if I don't like what my mother has cooked, I'm just going to order something of my liking with two easy clicks. If the dining table is multigenerational then it is likely that you will find multiple cuisines on it. Some are eating in a plate, and others are eating out of a box. And all this is while being on the same dining table. These small things become potential zones of conflict.

DECISION MAKING AND PRIORITIZATION

The one thing I feel younger generation is not learning well from its previous generations is the ability to discern between what is important and what is not. Older generations have that knack of discerning the important from trivial. And hence they focus and apply their attention and attempts on what is needed as opposed to what is desired. This keeps them often ahead in the game whereas, those who are unable to discern between the two are always chasing and are out of breath. Members of younger generations are often unable to decide and prioritize and hence feel that everything is important and are unable to prioritize properly. In this age of stiff competition and an obsession to always be busy, members of younger generation find no other alternative but to get dragged in the current. Now while the younger generation is living a lifestyle that is unhealthy and one that the older generation does not approve, the older generation often forget their contribution in creating and approving and voting for the creation of such an ecosystem. Regardless, this is another area of contention that is becoming front and center in multigenerational homes.

Now that you have learned about some major areas of conflict in multi-generational homes, I want to share the story of a unique issue in a multi-generational home. While it will amuse you, it will also highlight how the most mundane thing can become a source of pain in a multigenerational home. And it will also give you an opportunity to think about some instances that you may have experienced, which must have been unique and equally amusing.

THE STORY OF THE MICROWAVE

A professor and his wife were used to being empty nesters for a decade now in the Midwest region of the US. Due to the sudden onslaught of the Pandemic and the arrival of a second grandchild, the professor's home which was used to housing two individuals now housed six individuals. This is where the story of the microwave begins. And bear in mind that the protagonist of this story is the microwave. For the past many years of its existence our hero, the microwave, was an inane fly on the wall in the household. But it suddenly and unimaginably became the center of attention and agony for the multigenerational household.

While the professor was enjoying his newly earned retirement, his wife, his daughter, and his son-in-law worked from home. All the three had their individual rooms and workspaces. Although the professor had retired just a few months back, he still had a book project he was working on but his requirements for a workspace were not as stringent as the other three because he didn't have meetings and all. He too had his office and two other workspaces that he used alternatively.

One fine day, the professor, just like he had for the last 40 years, goes to the kitchen to warm up his coffee in the microwave. In the most unusual stroke of zemblanity, his son-in-law experiences a drop in his internet connection at the exact same moment. To not make this story any longer than it should be, a strong connection between the running of the microwave and the dropping of the internet connection was made by the son-in-law. So, the next time professor used his microwave, his son-in-law came running out requesting his not to turn on the microwave because it was somehow interfering with his internet. The professor immediately stopped the microwave. This was only the beginning.

For the next 1 year, the professor had to endure a silent unscientific and illogical restriction on the usage of microwave during working hours. This meant no luxury of warming up coffee, water, tea, food, and more for him. His microwave, which was a source of comfort suddenly became the equivalent of the unachievable goal of immortality. He could see it in front of him but could not use it. Imagine when you are forbidden to use microwave for a year in your own home. It can get challenging in many ways. I found this entire episode very amusing and had a hearty laugh when I was told this story.

The microwave here is just a tiny symbol for the types and magnitudes of adjustments one must make when cohabiting a multigenerational home. There are so many other things where adjustments need to be made.

CONCLUSION

In conclusion, I can say that there are many factors that have a strong potential to bring family as a unit back in its multigenerational form. And I find this potential desirable for the overall wellbeing of the human civilization. But at the same time, I am also fairly confident that the dynamics of any multigenerational home will not be what they were a century ago. Social, cultural, economic, privacy, relational equations have dramatically changed due to the introduction of technology, change in time, disintegration of the larger joint family system, and this will not allow for the past to be our future as is. Hypothetically, if there was a way to eliminate technology and other advances that foster the independence of an individual from the equation there is a possibility that the natural and a person's first group will come together to collaborate to survive. But then there is no chance of undoing any of the comfort increasing amenities and therefore this way will never ever actualize.

The roommate culture with limited interaction is the one that I personally feel will be the most difficult to overcome. Once a person gets used to space and quiet, their tolerance for the absence of it goes tremendously down. Moreover, there is a natural reactance to putting yourself in uncomfortable situations and when they emerge some short fuses are bound to go off. This means that there will be conflicts arising from expectations and for proper IH to be established, expectations will need to strongly be kept in check. Expectation management will be key to ensuring that a multigenerational family stays together with the shared goal of harmony and the wellbeing of everyone involved.

6

GOVERNMENT

The year 2024 is the most important year in the history of democratic governance. 64 countries are going to hold their general elections in 2024.[1] Billions of people are going to vote to choose their next installment of elected leaders. This will be pretty much the last time when the members of the silent generation will be participating in elections. The sun is also beginning to set on the role of Baby Boomers in governing and governance. Generational notions of trust, freedom, privacy, religiosity, liberal values, foreign policy, national security, and more are going to go through a tug-of-war. Environment in my humble opinion should be the big arena where generational conflicts will and should be seen. The younger generations are much more pro-environment, but they don't have the clout yet to bring in new legislations. With that said, it is also possible that they behave no differently than their predecessors once they are in those positions. Such is the nature of politics and governance.

In the next US election, there will be almost none or may be a few members from the silent generation. They are either physically and mentally unfit or are dead. Fewer and fewer are going to run for office from the Baby Boomer generation as well. This marks a huge shift in the approach and ideology with which the government system runs. These were the individuals who had seen the great depression, failing of the League of Nations, and participated in the second world war. It is the baby boomers and Gen Xers that are going to hold the lion's share of governance power.

Combined experiences of a given generation shapes and influences its approaches and attitudes toward issues and systems, which expose new areas of generational conflicts. The experiences of baby boomers and generation X are going to now reach its peak influencing ability with their numbers growing in the policy making seats. Gen Z does not hold much sway in the policy making yet, but it is exerting its pressure through their disruptive startups and technologies. The drastic changes they are bringing to the ecosystem are pushing the lawmakers to their boundaries. Let us look at some of the issues that are the possible grounds for generational clashes.

ENVIRONMENT AND CLIMATE

Environment and climate are an area where approaches, attitudes and subsequent policies differ which can lead to major generational conflicts. Due to the direness of the situation, and the longer vested interest in the planet the younger generation is extremely concerned as well as active in this area. A member of the Gen. Z generation making a huge impact single handedly, and in the process influencing policies in many countries across the globe is Greta Thunberg. Greta has taken on the Goliath task and has thus far shown tremendous resilience and perseverance. The younger generations are still emotionally connected to nature and our planet, which I personally believe is the way to be. They don't see the planet as an entity which exists to exploit and empty. They see our planet as our only option to survive and they look at other plants and animals as cohabitants.

The above is not exactly the viewpoint among the older generations such as the baby boomers and Gen. X. Their generational experiences of major events during their formative years have influenced them in their attitude and approach toward the nature and the planet. In some ways they are still trying to conquer the planet and its resources. Based on all the environmental degradation and manipulation that we have seen it is safe to assume that they feel less hesitant in ignoring certain environmental destruction and in allowing the exploitation of nature to happen right under their noses. The decrease in the percentage of natural and wild flora and fauna is terribly disappointing. It is the younger generation that has to toil hard to increase the natural biodiversity and bring it to a proportion that is not detrimental to the human race. The younger generations are now more concerned and less afraid to ask the difficult questions pertaining to development and progress coming at a certain cost which their generation is unwilling to pay. There is one thing to note over here that the lifestyles of the younger generation are not entirely walking the talk at the moment. Their consumption and indulgence in material items as well as the need to express their identity through different external expressions also comes at a cost to the environment. These things do undermine their concerns to a degree and send conflicted messages to the other generations.

This is also one among the many reasons why the older generations do not take the younger generations seriously.

The older generation, on the other hand never realized when their need to secure the future of their kins would itself come at the cost of jeopardizing the very future of their kins. There was definitely a lack of foresight and an increased level of greed, but it might be slightly unfair to go to the level of categorizing them as evil. While they understood the significance of compounding in the financial sense, they did not apply the same principle of compounding while ravaging the planet of its resources. This blind spot of theirs has costed human civilization a lot. The changes in the weather and climate are felt all across the globe. Keeping up with the spirit of polarization that humans are demonstrating globally, the climate too is becoming more and more polarized. We are seeing extremes everywhere. And extremes are not good for human survival. Humans survive and flourish in moderation.

One example of extreme is the fact that agencies and experts have had to come together to decide whether they need a new rating for hurricanes. Hurricanes are categorized based on their severity from 1 to 5. However, in the last couple of years hurricanes have demonstrated capabilities that are matching the qualifiers for the upper end of the category 5 hurricane and more. The current categories are not sufficient to provide proper understanding about the extent of damage and the level of evacuation and rebuilding capacities needed. Hence it is likely that very soon we will have an entirely new category, which is the category 6 of hurricanes. Another statistic that made me very sad was something that I heard from Sir David Attenborough he said that only 4% of the mammalian mass is unmanipulated by humans.[2] 96% of the mammalian mass on the planet is manipulated and controlled by humans. For how long can we continue abusing our nature is a big question mark in governments? It might be possible that party affiliation may not remain as strong when it comes to this issue, and generational affiliations may outweigh the affiliation to a party. We have seen a trailer of this happening in the US Congress. There was a conflict in approaches between the leader of the party who was also the speaker of the house and four new members of congress. The four belonged to a younger generation and wanted to do things in a new age way. This brought generational conflict within the party. What is worth noticing is that the leader of the party was a female, and the four new members of congress were also females. You would normally believe that females in congress especially from the same party who want the same thing would not get into a conflict as this conflict is good for no one. But it happened. Lack of IH was the reason for it. It was unfortunate because together they would have been a force to reckon with but then due to the lack of IH they could not collaborate and contribute to the very thing they all were passionate for.

ARTIFICIAL INTELLIGENCE

Artificial intelligence is a very tricky category. I say this because it very closely aligns with the issues pertaining to environment and climate as well as with the issues pertaining to trust and integrity. You may wonder why, and I hope to give you a good understanding in the coming paragraphs as to why artificial intelligence is connected in the hip with both these issues. Artificial intelligence becomes important for us because it is a technology and there is a generational divide around comfort with technology and its usage. Let me first highlight the relation of artificial intelligence with climate and planet. Artificial intelligence is a type of very sophisticated processing with almost unlimited abilities. However, the processing has to happen somewhere, and the processing also requires some form of energy to run. So how is artificial intelligence using planetary resources to keep its heart beating? Let's begin with water. Fresh water is very important for the large data processing and computing plants to keep them cool. For this they only use fresh water. The simple role of the fresh water is to ensure that these centers do not overheat. It has now been noted in news articles that freshwater areas in the vicinity of artificial intelligence development centers have seen a substantial spike in the usage by these enterprises. In times when fresh water, especially potable water, is scarce and there are still billions of people on this planet who don't have access to clean drinking water, is the use of water for cooling these plants justified? At what cost are we again indulging in the research and progress that comes from artificial intelligence.

The second aspect that pertains to climate and planet is in the very mind of artificial intelligence. As compared to a simple search done on a search engine as opposed to any search done on any of the large language models that use machine learning and artificial intelligence, the latter utilizes much more energy. This gap in energy consumption is right now bearable. But as the large language models grow in size and their usage becomes commercialized or democratized then this is going to cause a serious imbalance going further. Right now, a search on a large language model utilizes four times more energy than a simple Google search. We don't have the capacities to keep the mind and the heart of artificial intelligence running, the mind being its processing and the heart being its processing plants need to be cooled.

I hope this gives you some understanding about the complexity of the issue at hand. We still have the second aspect of trust and integrity to discuss. Democracy and the democratic process is in peril because of artificial intelligence inspired technologies. The ability of large language models and artificial intelligence related technologies to generate videos, generate personas, generate speeches, generate advertisements, and make them seem extremely real is dangerous to the free and fair process of election. Fake news, deep fakes, and other technologies when weaponized can severely shake the trust of the people in the elected leaders and the democratic process. And the implications of this goes above and beyond a student having his or her or their essay written by an artificial intelligence technology and passing the class. Any kind of election failure or a civil conflict comes at a huge cost throwing a country behind by decades. So, this is why it becomes an issue where generational synergy is utmost important. Younger generations are heavily engaged in the creation of these technologies and in this case, it is the older generation that is asking the tough questions or putting some kind of resistance against the blind development of technologies. The environmental impact of artificial intelligence is unknown at this moment and there is one bill that has been introduced in the US senate to mandate companies to disclose the level of environmental impact that their artificial intelligence technologies have. Similarly in many other countries blind adoption of these technologies should be prevented, especially from a cybersecurity point of view. These technologies are not entirely full proof at the moment and the engineers and the people behind it are working to ensure that they become foolproof but then there is no assurance at any given point that they are free of any vulnerabilities.

SOCIAL MEDIA

Recently, I spent some time watching a senate hearing of all five major social media companies' leaders. It is clear that from their point of view they are only providing good services with noble intentions and are also ensuring the basic hygiene to the best of their abilities. However, I felt compelled to challenge my thinking if not entirely change it when one of the senators alluded to the fact that the largest social media platform is also the largest platform for selling girls and indulge in trafficking. This might have been an unintended outcome of the services offered. This may have not even been thought of when thinking of all the possibilities of what people could do on social media sites, but it is a reality. A recent social media addition to the world of sexually explicit material disseminating service is OnlyFans, who has had constant run-ins with the government and policy makers because of the content generated by minors and purchased subsequently. It has also been proven that foreign powers have used social media to cause disruptive protests and civil unrest in numerous countries including the US. These were not the issues that previous generation of lawmakers had to deal with. But the current generation of law makers who have very little understanding of the technology or the output of it are having to draft laws about these. How do you draw a map if the boundaries keep changing?

Government and lawmakers have the ability to shut down social media. The most populous country on the planet, India, banned one of the fastest growing social media companies. TikTok was banned by India. 1.4 billion people are unable to freely use TikTok.[3] Now India did not ban TikTok for the reasons of not being able to understand the technology or not being able to support it with its connectivity infrastructure. It banned it because of the reasons of national security and protecting its data. But this is not new. Many nations have bans on many social media platforms. Russia, China, the Middle East have all put barriers on the use of social media platforms. However, these countries put a ban to protect the interests of the government and not necessarily the nation at large, which does not seem to be the case with India. On the one hand, these bans are protecting the status quo but on the other hand are also preventing their own citizens from keeping up with the world and to communicate freely without any fear.

This is the tragedy of our times. Without generational synergy it will be impossible to take care of this tragedy and we will eventually transform this tragedy into a Tempest. How to draft regulations for something that is not static? Social media just like the world of technology is evolving superfast. It is tremendously dynamic. It wants to encroach each and every possible aspect of human life and endeavor. And sadly, in this case it is not just the younger generations that are spending a whole lot of time on it, it is also the older generations. Everyone has something for them in this large virtual system to keep them engaged and occupied. The older generation may not use Snapchat, but they are spending crazy amounts of time on WhatsApp. What they don't know is that much of what they see on WhatsApp is generated and circulated from the other social media applications that they choose not to sign up for.

Everything has jurisdictions, everything has limits, and everything has boundaries. It is only this world of social media where the boundaries are fluid, transparent, and permeable. The tendency to share private information and make it available for public consumption is not something that was a common trait among the people 20 years ago. People believed in keeping their life private but now those very same people are willingly providing so much information for open public consumption. There is a clear need for the generations here to come together because they are both victims and perpetrators at the same time to ensure that this space becomes free of abuse and maleficence. Honesty is where it should all start.

GENERATIONAL UPRISING

Millennials and Gen Z are very much in favor of liberal, democratic, and shared governance. This approach went directly against several autocratic regimes in the Middle East and South America. In all these countries we have seen tragic civil wars. Protests that were facilitated by social media plagued many nations. Radical communicative actions became common occurrences. Arab Spring was a series of conflicts where many autocratic governments were overturned. In some cases, the autocratic leader of the government was ruling supreme for more than two decades. Such leaders were either put behind bars or killed. If you come to think of it two out of the top three economies in the world have had the leader for more than two decades. For how long they will be able to hold on to such uncontested powers is the question. Will they give way to a different generation voluntarily or will they also be pushed out in a violent manner. IH can facilitate a smooth succession of power and avoid violence.

IH can open doors for inclusivity and participation. Transfer of power does not have to be ugly or violent. It is the real hallmark not just of a form of government but also life and evolution in general. The power grab is so competitive everywhere that there is hardly any effort made in government settings to groom and prepare individuals for leading nations. Everyone who gets the job of leading a nation sadly learns it on the job. For most other professions, one has to have some training, apprenticeship, residency, internship, etc. where they are given opportunities to try to test their abilities and skills in ensuring individual capability in doing justice to the position. However, when it comes to leading a nation, no one is ever prepared and once in the position, the willingness to leave disappears. The general distrust on other generations' ability to do good for the nation is a staple of the generation in position of leadership.

GENERATIONS BASED ON DEVELOPMENT

Looking at the age of people in the government is one way to look at generations. But there are always other ways of looking at generations that open up new perspective and priorities. In governments at the level of a nation there is another way to look at generations. And this is on the basis of development and income. There is a group of nations that are developed and have high per capita income. This group of nation belongs in a generational grouping which are pushing for a pause on manufacturing, nuclear programs, keeping a check on carbon emissions, reduce drilling and exploration of natural resources, declare more and more regions of planet as sanctuaries, and more. The developed generation of nations are the ones who have already exploited the natural resources to the maximum. That is how they are in the developed positions. This generation is mostly made up of European countries and the US along with a few others. These countries have not only exploited natural resources as stated earlier but have also colonized and exploited other nations and territories for their singular gains. This generation now wants to be the wise one and provide counsel to the nations and be there for them to solve their problems.

The second generation of nations are the ones that got their freedom from their colonizers between 1940s and 1960s. This generation is now on a manufacturing spree and is the largest base for consumptions. What their consumption lacks in per capita quantity is made up through their large numbers. The first generation does not have a large population, but their consumption is out of the roof in comparison to the other two generations. They are the ones who are saying that don't tell us that we are exploiting nature. You exploited it to your heart's full and now you are wearing the hat of a moral police when you have no moral ground or any authority to tell us anything. We have a responsibility to feed our growing population and for that we have to indulge in manufacturing, which comes at a cost. While we are trying to balance that cost, we most certainly don't want to listen to your sermons. The major generational conflict is between this generation of countries and the ones that are developed in regard to many legal, policy, environment, and denuclearization. The constitution of the United Nation's Security Council and its permanent members is a matter of big generational conflict.

The generation of nations who are now making up a large chunk of population and are responsible for the flow of money are arguing that for how long will countries that either don't have our best interest in their minds or the ones that don't represent us will keep making decisions on our behalf. How come we don't have a permanent voice in the security council. Why should we let others keep making decisions on our behalf. Five decades ago, we were young and despite being independent we may have needed some handholding. But we don't need that anymore because we know what will happen to us if we follow your path. We don't want to end up like you. Moreover, our character is very different, and we want to progress and evolve in tandem to our core essence and not in the way some of you have. This conflict is brewing and will escalate in the next decade.

The third and final generation are the ones that are extremely underdeveloped and poor. These nations are barely trying to survive day by day. Their issues are more of the freedom from basics. Many are experiencing internal violent clashes and are fighting ideological and religious colonization. This generation has a seat on the table but no voice. They are mere puppets to the geographically nearest first-generation nations. The moment a strong leader emerges in any of these countries, their economy is destabilized, and the voice of the leader is silenced. With the anticipated youth bulge centered in these nations this is where the power will shift. We have already started hearing that the power is moving from North to South and from the West to the East. Both the North and the West are going to try tooth and nail to hold on to their power and grip over global ecosystem. For the West and North to retain its supremacy, it will have to somehow convince its populations to go on a path of major downgrading their consumption and quality of life. It cannot continue to consume in excess and then tell other to not do the same. How will their internal generations react to such requests is yet to be seen. Two factors that could have successfully encouraged people to downgrade would have been religion and family but they both are suffering a crisis of faith and a crisis of drifting apart. Surely the corporations are not going to endorse that message. The only remaining player is education and with the declining significance of humanities and arts, and increase in STEM focus, there is very little chance that education has the gravitas to convince. It might even be able to convey but I highly doubt that it can convince its population to downgrade their lifestyles.

National conflicts based on generation of development one belongs to is also the result of lack of IH. IH can certainly be encouraged through diplomacy and exchanges. But it can be hastened much through honesty and shared governance in drafting of global regulations and legislations to conduct ourselves to ensure the health and wellbeing of our planet.

CONCLUSION

In conclusion I say that while 2024 is a very important year for democracy due to the 64 general elections, this year is when the generational change and take over begins. The younger generation abounding in optimism for future, concern for ecosystem, and enabled by social technologies is going to emerge as a powerful challenger to the generational status quo. Older generations will have to either start collaborating or start making way for the younger more active and seemingly more conscientious and transparent generation. Despite the innumerable advances, happiness has not pervaded in the lives of people, and this is the biggest failure of government. This is what is going to be challenged ferociously by the younger generation. One of the biggest reasons for conflict will be that younger generations don't recognize authority but more importantly they are seeing older generation with more and more hostility as the perpetrators of greed and exploitation.

As usual, I strongly caution against discarding the older generation in the governments because they know how the government machinery works. The older generation knows how much powerless those in power are. Even if the younger generation wins the seats, they will have to work with the older generations to understand how the machinery of government works and how can they make it work for them. Otherwise, despite greater numbers younger generations will not be able to accomplish much.

Harmony in government between generations and between generations of nation will enable and actualize harmony with nature. If the generations keep arguing, then we will miss out on the larger agenda. Generational schisms must be avoided at all costs, because a slow-moving machine cannot afford breakdowns. And without IH there will be breakdowns. IH in government is the crucial block of votes that are willing to and able to go beyond the party lines to make the impossible possible.

NOTES

1.   Ewe, K. (2023). The ultimate election year: All the elections around the World in 2024. *Time Magazine*. https://time.com/6550920/world-elections-2024/
2.   Attenborough, D. (2020). A life on our planet. https://scrapsfromtheloft.com/movies/david-attenborough-a-life-on-our-planet-transcript/
3.   Vanjani, K. (2024). India banned TikTok. Then Instagram and other Copy-cats Took Off. https://www.barrons.com/articles/india-banned-tiktok-meta-1b0465bd

7

RELIGION

Organized religion is going through a crisis of recruitment and retention. The roots of this crisis are set in the sheer lack of generational synergy. The generational divide is really polarized when it comes to religion. Traditionally, religion has played a crucial role in bringing people together. Religion has not only brought people together but also brought the different generations together. The older generation would ensure that the younger generation was as involved in the religious traditions and practices to ensure continuity. And this continuity has stayed intact for centuries but the last 30 years have changed the dynamics of the continuity.

Generational continuity of involvement and engagement with religion and religious practices has undergone a change. To a great degree this discontinuity can be credited to the wrongdoings directed toward members of younger generations by the leaders therein. In the last 30 years, major scandals pertaining to abuse, exploitation, misuse have come to the light, which have triggered a dissent from religion and its practices.

Gen. Z and millennials are losing interest in religion. Globally, it is more common, and maybe even popular for young adults to say that I am spiritual. A large majority suddenly wants to identify with spirituality and eschew being religious. The shift from religious to spiritual has reached a stage where to be religious is now a matter of soft taboo. There prevails a stigma in the public square about being openly and vehemently religious. The semantics of the word religious have changed to mean to someone who is narrow-minded, and a cause of many social problems.

There is a constant difficulty of not finding young people in religious worships and places. Every religion is struggling in fighting this uphill battle. Religions have even gone online and streaming their services to accommodate the changing behaviors of the believers, but even that is not working fully. I remember reading this maybe half a decade or so ago. It could have been a fake news, but this made my day back then. The news item said that get the same blessings as if you were in person by following the Pope on Twitter. I don't know about others, but this delighted me because I saw openness to a different approach to keep people in the fold. All the forces that suffocated people are being loosened and people are still slipping away. By no means, I am saying that this is bad or good. I am merely noticing the move and trying to bring to attention the evolving trend.

WHO IS RELIGION FOR?

Who is religion for is the fundamental question that is driving people away, especially members of younger generation from it. Directly or indirectly, I have asked this question to countless folks during my travels in four different continents and based on the different responses and my reflections on them, I have narrowed down the following themes of broad perspectives that become the basis for providing a response to the above question. All these perspectives have generational implications and therefore it is important that we expose ourselves to them. Well, the people who are custodians of a religion undoubtedly say that religion is for everyone. But there is an apparent conflict of interest there so instead, let us look at the other perspectives.

ABLE-UNABLE

A straightforward and pragmatic perspective on who is religion for tells us that religion is for those who are unable. Unable and able is a spectrum largely based on how well an individual can manage his or her or their life and its intricacies on their own. Able people do not need religion because they can manage life and its intricacies without structured guidance. It is the people who are unable to manage life and its intricacies for whatever reason that need religion. Religion provides a structure to conduct life. Religion provides a template on how to live life and remain afloat in different situations.

It is important to note that no person is fully able or fully unable. The same person can be able in one phase of his or her or their life and then can also be unable in a different phase of his or her or their life. So, depending on whether a person is able or unable at a given point of time in his or her or their life, religion can be for them or not. This begs a further question that is someone entirely able at any point of time? There are two perspectives about this. The first perspective suggests that no one can be fully able at any given point of time. There are always aspects of life in which one is unable while simultaneously being able in other aspects at the very same time. From that standpoint, religion is for a person regardless of what phase of life he or she or they are in. The counter perspective here claims that a person cannot be unable if he or she or they do not care about certain aspects of life or certain aspects don't bother them at that given point. For example, a young adult does not have to worry much about retirement problems, or the health issues connected with old age. Similarly, an older person does not have to worry about the insecurities pertaining to education and securing first job like the younger members. Hence, if we adopt this approach then a person can be fully able at a given point of time in life and not in need of religion.

CHOICE

An entirely different way to look at this question is from the perspective of agency. Agency here mostly refers to the person's ability to choose. In other words, religion is for those who can choose. Is religion a matter of choice? While most would argue positively, I wonder if that is the ground reality. How many really have a choice in choosing if religion is for them or not. As soon as you are born you are categorized and placed in the same religion as your parents and are even subjected to the many rituals and traditions. By the time you become aware and mature to choose, you are way too much invested in one religion and that makes it challenging to move on to a different one or entirely away from it. There are some people who have succeeded in doing so but they are far and few. So, who chooses who? Does a religion choose a person, or a person chooses a religion? There is also the added nuance of choosing between religions or choosing options beyond religions too. Religion, till the 20th century, has been the prime example of generational loyalty. There are millions of people on the planet who are part of a religion that members of their family seven or ten or even hundred generations ago were. Such loyalty is rarely seen in any other facet of choice making. And this is keeping the consideration that there have been upheavals and forced changes that have been made over the years. For a large majority, religion is a default.

TIME

Third perspective on who is religion for stems from the availability and unavailability of time. This perspective suggests that people who have time can afford to utilize it or waste it on religion. For those people who are busy and do not have time, religion is not for them. Religion requires time commitment. There are multiple activities, rituals, and traditions which need to be followed and enjoyed as part of a religious tradition. With the modern-day puritan lifestyle where in work takes the lion's share of an individual's time it is very difficult to provide time for religious activities. While some managed to do this the juggling act is not easy.

In many cases religion is nothing but something to do during the weekend. An hour every weekend is more than sufficient but anything more or beyond that becomes a burden on the time commitment. How do you understand life and its dependence and correlation with the time is a critical question. Religion is something that only people with time can afford to indulge in. Which generation do you think is rich in time? Some generations manage their time much better than others. If you are from the generation that manages time well then you can be a participant in the myriad activities and worship practices. Do baby boomers have more time or does the Gen Z have more time? What about the generations in between. Baby boomers and Gen X are much more settled financially and socially in relation to Gen Z. Technically the Silent generation should have the maximum time but then they don't have the physical ability to do things as much as they like.

NEED FOR STRUCTURE

Every individual has a distinct need for structure in life. Some thrive when there is structure, and some feel suffocated when there is structure. Religion provides a structure for people to follow. And hence religion is for people who require structure in their life. It is the presence of this structure that keeps them oriented toward the path of goodness. On their own they don't trust themselves enough to remain on the path of goodness. On the contrary, there is another group that feels stifled when they must operate and conduct themselves within the confines of a structure. Their need for structure is negligible and is contrary to their individual progress. They argue that the very God who created the universe and religion does not have any structure so why we must adhere to one that is mostly curated by other humans. Based on the reasoning of this perspective, it is logical to suggest that religion is for those generations who prefer structure in their life.

The structure point also touches upon aspects of managing freedom. If a person has full freedom to curate his or her or their day and life then it is possible that while some can come up with positive options to occupy themselves, others will not be able to occupy themselves positively and will succumb to the devil of boredom and end up causing more damage to their own self and the society around. Religion provides a routine and a list of daily activities that need to be performed. These activities are helpful in keeping you from getting bored and succumbing to situations where things get out of hand. Every religion offers suggestions on what one needs to do every waking hour of life. A big portion of this is spent in remembering God and chanting his or her or their name.

SCIENCE

Another perspective argues that God is not for those who believe in science. The people who believe in God don't believe in science. Such false binaries are held strongly among people. Science here is more of a symbol of autonomy, courage, taking charge, strength, and conviction. The argument here is that for a person of science there is no mystery. For example, they can articulate exactly why rain falls. Rain does not mean the wrath of a God and hence don't have to resort to praying to fictional gods who punish through excessive rain.

The contrarian approach suggests that science is the only way of producing knowledge and other ways are flawed and unreliable. Religion is for those who want to continue to believe in and live by knowledge that is flawed and unreliable. But for those who are unlike that, religion is not for them. Such binaries are hard to counter and reason with. In addition to science, modernity is another perspective that helps answer the question who is religion for? An individual who identifies with modernity eschews religiosity.

CONFORMITY AND CREATIVITY

This is yet another perspective that provides us with an answer to the question who is religion for? The wide understanding here is that people who are conformists are the ones who religion is for. This is because in their opinion religion does not change, religion does not evolve. It only and eternally keeps conforming with the past. Religion does not show any indication of how things can be different. Religion does not like change. Religion does not like creativity. Instead of supporting these, religion has always stood against and in the way of creative expressions. Unless creativity has been utilized in alignment with the goals of a religion, creativity and creative people have been shut down, and even imprisoned and killed.

Creativity and creative endeavors led to the era of enlightenment followed by renaissance. If not for religion this era would have dawned centuries before. Creative individuals have been the one who have systematically introduced thoughts and devices that have made human life better. Whereas conformists have done the exact opposite they have not introduced any new thoughts or devices that's altered the state of human life for good. Religion here is looked like a static mechanism and therefore those with a conformist mindset are able to better adjust to the form and function of religion. A creative individual, on the other hand, is simply not able to excel within the form and function of a religion. Generationally who is creative and who is conformist?

The history of religion messing with the people who were creative and dared to confess the truth has left a deep scar on the generations to come. Anything that deviated from the norm or in other words was extraordinary, was labeled as deviant and marked for extermination. This is also the reason witches were hunted and burned alive. Witches refused to confirm to others' religion and continued their belief. Since this is more about the generational perspective, the younger generation is modern and therefore doesn't believe that religion is for them whereas, the older generation is less modern and hence religion is for them. While creative individuals are not meant for religion and religion is also not meant for them, there is a catch here. The catch is that while religion may not be for creative people, spirituality for sure is. In a later part of this chapter, I will provide a more elaborate discussion on the role of creativity in spirituality and religion.

Let us engage you now in this dialog. It is important that you also realize how and where you stand with these considerations and binaries. There are two questions in the Table 1 below. The first question is who do you think religion is for? There are 12 groups and for each you have to say yes or no. If you feel that religion, for example, is not for scientific people then you say NO, and if you think religion is for scientific people then you say YES.

In the Question two, you must categorize where do people of a given category fall in. For example, there are more creative people in younger generation then you say YES in the space given under younger generation. This is a self-assessment to see where you stand. Based on this you can work on

Table 1. Assessing Self-Biases Pertaining to Religion.

Q1: Is Religion For?		Q2: Members of Which Generation Are More...?	
	Yes/No	Older Generation	Younger Generation
Able			
Unable			
Creative			
Conformists			
Scientific			
Unscientific			
In high need of structure			
In low need of structure			
With a choice			
With no choice			
Time rich			
Time poor			

yourself in the areas where you find that you are being biased or opinionated or unnecessarily judgmental.

Unless you are an exception, your answers are indicative of what I am going to talk about next. It is because of these understandings that a certain phenomenon is being seen globally.

THE MASS EXODUS

The movement away from religion is what I refer to as the Mass Exodus of the 21st century. For this book, I made it a point to interact with different stakeholders of the mass exodus from religion. As noted in an earlier chapter, Christianity is losing younger generation due to several reasons such as scandals, abuse, lack of being able to connect, anachronistic practices, and more. The younger generations of the West are more and more being attracted by Eastern religions and are practicing them. According to an estimate, there are 10 million Christians that are practicing Buddhism. It is not that the Buddhist monasteries are filled with young people. This is just a jump from one structure to another that seems less constricting. And do note that this happens a lot among young adults and older adults whose lifestyles and life events stray away from the set normal. What they do is jump from one church to another. So, there is moving within the same religion, across religions, and there is also the complete disaffiliation from religion.

Through conversations and interactions with many such individuals, I have surmised that they are not necessarily upset or disappointed with God or even to some extent their religion greatly. They are upset with the older generation that has sinned against the faith. The older generation is insisting on upholding a self-serving hegemon. They have not been able to be a role model to the younger generation that can inspire faith. Instead, what they have achieved is that now members of the younger generation and even slightly older genera-tions, which would be parents, are full of suspicion toward anything religion. The clothes and symbols that once upon a time were symbols of unwavering trust and surrender are now the symbols of deceit and greed. It has come to a point where stand-up comedians are also able to effectively use religion and GOD as a topic of mockery and ridicule. My insights on the mass exodus, mainly the one where the angst is toward the custodians of the religion and not God, will be the key to restoring faith in religion. To give you a birds-eye view of the conversations and interviews, I will share three. These three conversa-tions happened with a couple in rural Ohio in USA, an Australian chaplain in Europe, and an octogenarian former nun of a religious order.

The Australian chaplain and I were riding on a train that was headed up a mountain in Europe. The incline was very steep, so the train was moving slowly. I was introduced to a girl in her early thirties. I was told that she is pursuing her doctoral degree. This made me interested in learning about her dissertation topic. As it turned out, this girl was a chaplain in Australia, who was pursuing a doctoral degree, and was researching transformation and change. While listening to the chaplain describe the major theory and meth-odology of the dissertation, I sensed some unease. Being used to trusting my gut, I disclosed to her that I felt some discomfort and unease in her voice. The chaplain looked at me intently and then revealed what she referred to as her inner tempest. I will not go into all the details here, but the highlights are as follows: the mis-actions of the clergy in a certain city of Australia were deeply bothering this chaplain. Hundreds of millions were paid just in one city of Australia as recompensation, and much more will be paid, she added, as more mis-actions will be uncovered. The partner of our chaplain was also a chap-lain, and both were born in a family of priests and clergy. Our chaplain was greatly disturbed by the quandary within and there was deep melancholy and dilemma to continue or quit. While there was disappointment toward God for letting little children suffer, the angst was not against God. The angst in this case was exclusively against the mis-actions of the custodians.

Across the globe in rural Ohio, I met a couple who had spent three decades of their life working in a trans-national organization, whose mandate was to share the gospel throughout the world. I was driving this couple on a leisurely drive to Niagara Falls. This is when we had a full day to ourselves where we talked all things life. One thing we talked at length was their role in serving an institution that they believed was doing good by spreading the gospel to those who were not aware of it. However, they said that they were definitely done. They have done enough behind the scenes work to know that much of the work is not worth it. Giving God to people is one thing but then putting those very same people under the charge of their local shepherds was an entirely different hustle. In their life, post being disillusioned, what was the most difficult for them I wondered was how challenging it must have been for them to have dedicated three decades believing in something and doing things for the spread of it, and now having to live with those three decades as the greatest mistake of their life. This type of realization is incredibly difficult to reconcile. Their past continues to follow them in uncanny ways. Their rectification and course correction puts their credibility and loyalty in question. They become easy targets of the ad Hominem fallacy attacks, if not to their face, then for sure behind their backs. Unlike our Australian chaplain, this couple interestingly has not only turned away from givers of God but also from God.

Last, I speak of a former colleague. Little did I know about my colleague when she was my colleague. My interaction with her was restricted to her walking into my office to tend to my plants. After recognizing how awful my plants were doing despite my taking care of them, she decided to take things in her hand. It was much later that I realized that she was a nun or a sister in one of the orders within catholic system. During one of our lengthy and in-depth conversation, I realized that she has been a nun for the past 60 years of her life. She had contributed every penny of what she had earned in all these years to the mount and the church. But now when she was about to retire at the age of 80, she was unwilling to continue. She had to send in an application which eventually goes all the way up to the Pope where he formally must excuse her from her obligations of her lifelong vow. I asked her that what was the reason for letting go of what you had done for the past 60 years? Moreover, it is now that you will need the help and support of a system and infrastructure that will take care of you and feed you and tend to you as you age. In the world out there, you are alone. Her short response was that I want to live life. Nothing about my faith is going to change but I don't need the rules and regulations to keep me faithful. They are stifling my spirituality. In this case the person has not given up God but has abandoned the rules and lifestyle set by the custodians of God. To me she sings the song of a free bird.

These three instances should give you some idea about the different struggles at different stages of life. Based on the countless many that I have interviewed and interacted with, I can tell for sure that there is a mass exodus happening. There is no single reason for this mass exodus and that is what makes this complicated. For many there is a single event that sowed the seed of their departure from religion. For many that was never the case. They simply drifted apart and never returned.

If you are interested more in learning about the religious disaffiliation in America it is worth spending time reading the brief report titled, "Gen Z and the Future of Faith in America" by Daniel Cox. His report indicates that Gen Z has the highest members that remain unaffiliated to any religion at 34% as opposed to the meager 9% from the silent generation. Millennials and Gen Z show the highest disaffiliation rates among all generations. The report even suggests that the Gen X, which is the parenting and care giving generation to millennials and Gen Z has not done enough to ensure that their kids remain affiliated. This is also when a lot of scandals came out, so I don't blame them either for not being stricter with their kids when they themselves were not sure of who to trust and how much. There is another angle to why people have decided to disaffiliate themselves from faith. This angle is not very openly or elaborately spoken about. I will mention it briefly over here but not too much in detail because it does not have too much to do with Generations. Violence in the name of religion. Different kinds of violence have been observed all around the world either to defend a religion or to propagate a religion. Increasingly, there are generational followers that are tired of violence and want to disassociate from any and every kind of violence. People of faith when they see their religion as responsible for violence, they disaffiliate themselves from the religion.

SCIENCE AND KNOWING

Knowledge and wisdom have often been pitted against religion. Due to the internet and other technologies, humans that live today have unparalleled access to knowledge at their fingertips. Let me highlight that a cage match between science and religion is more of a western concept. Where I grew up and the religion that I grew up in, my religion was essentially a teaching tradition with the goal of enlightening oneself through thorough knowledge of the self. Science and knowing was the religion. On the contrary, the western knowledge systems were heavily suppressed by religion.

Our history is full of seeing beliefs gain prominence, lose prominence, disappear, and at times reappear. If you look at it, science has been known as the arch enemy of religion. This is probably why when religion was in power in West, it did practically everything possible and imaginable to suppress the rise of science. Instead of being an everyday occurrence, enlightenment became an era where science and knowledge had to sneak and survive in shadows. After Enlightenment came the period of Renaissance. It is after the Renaissance that the western world and the western religions saw a tremendous shift in the following as well as the nature of the following by the religious faithful.

Knowledge has contributed to eradicate false understandings and promises of religion, which we often refer to as Blind Faith. The Romans and the Greeks believed in God's, and we have substantial evidence of their beliefs and practices. However, even they don't believe in those Gods anymore. Comprehension, wisdom, and knowledge have contributed to this loss of faith. Similarly, a certain increment in the knowledge and understanding has also led to the disaffiliation of people from the Abrahamic religions.

SPIRITUALITY IS THE NEW RELIGION AND SELF IS THE NEW GOD

The West is bound to see a decline in religion. Not all regions are seeing this. Many are seeing an increase in religiosity too, but the gains are marginal. Due to secularization, democratization and capitalization of the society, God and religion have decreased in popularity. But not spirituality. As noted earlier in the chapter, spirituality is the new religion. Spirituality as a label or a framing is being steadily chosen over religious. This is especially true in the younger generations. My personal view on this is that due to the mixture of the discovery of scandals and abuse, and the inherent aversion toward structure and order in young adults has led to the mass exodus. It is when parents lose their persuasive ability and the ability to give answers disaffiliation at this level can happen. The sad part is that the custodians of religions have put the parents in a helpless situation and are now blaming them for not being able to influence their kids. Spirituality is a different beast altogether. It has no structure. It exclusively relies on an individual's inner will and most importantly creativity.

Spirituality is creativity in action. Spirituality has no rules or set guidelines for conducting oneself. As long as the individual recognizes that there is something beyond him or her or them and is in search to connect with it, he or she or they are spiritual. Spirituality does not require any real commitment. You can be spiritual without doing anything. You have the freedom to be as creative as you want. This creative freedom is what the younger generations are insanely attracted to. Spirituality does not ask for money, spirituality does not incite violence, spirituality does not make active efforts to increase it followership, spirituality does not consider you any less or more if you do something or not. All these are favored by the younger generations. Spirituality, much to my disapproval, also enables individual justification and rationalization of certain basic amoral compromises. In a realm of free spirit, rules don't exist, and this can work against an individual with a weak inner will.

As we noted earlier, how the Maslow's hierarchy was used to explain the role and positioning of God with changing generation. The most recent paradigm in that understanding was that God is in you. With the evolving spirituality that has changed to God is you. You and God are one. There is no distinction, there is no binary. Spirituality does help individual reach such conclusions. The paradigm of self is the new God and I embrace that God is the best model because there is no middleman. There is no custodian who can break my trust or abuse his position. There is no set of guidelines that I can be judged based on. I am in a zone where my creative spirit is free to soar. I am not bound, and I am instead free. Spirituality takes me toward freedom to actualize my creative potential.

CONCLUSION

Religion is experiencing generational disaffiliation. I cannot imagine, even if I try hard what religion will look like in the life of an individual two generations from now. I am certain that it will exist but in an extremely watered-down version. Religion was something that parents and grandparents gave their children. Now the giving ability of older generations is severely challenged. A major enterprise that has shaped our society is in the beginning stages of collapse. Without Intergenerational Harmony, it will be almost impossible to revive religion. And we certainly don't want to revive religion that puts breaks on knowledge and breeds on people's ignorance. Not everyone has the ability of poesis. And for those who don't have that ability to create something out of nothing, we need guidance. That guiding force is religion that has also shown the path to countless in dire need. By harnessing the power of Intergenerational Harmony, the good that is in religion can and must be retained.

8

GARNERING INTERGENERATIONAL HARMONY (IH)

By now it must be clear to you that IH is a major strategic and competitive advantage at so many levels. The return on investment is definitely much more and long-term. IH within family, religion, businesses/corporation, education, and government is going to be the critical catalyst that will increase efficiency, collaboration, action, and overall wellbeing of all. Without IH each of these sectors and enterprises within will be like a hamster in a wheel, with a lot of movement in the same place. As multigenerationality becomes a staple, IH becomes the cornerstone for a more balanced and equitable growth.

A society with high levels of IH will be the one to navigate the 21st century with relative ease. IH encourages everyone to have more patience toward a member of another generation. This, in turn, can not only create a friendly society but also reduce prejudice and bias. Keeping the biases in check will automatically reduce generational discrimination and increase generational collaboration. Cooperation becomes easy when there is harmony. This harmony-led cooperation prevents us from repeating mistakes of the past, which also saves us time and other resources.

Together, all the generations can become better stewards and champions of the environment and its inhabitants. One generation cannot achieve the goal of restoring ecological balance. Harmony between generations is critical for harmony with nature. Harmony between generations also provides the collaborative actions and enterprises a fresh and unique perspective along with technological superiority. When the tech savvy young generation works in collaboration with other generations and the resource rich older generations work with the tech savvy younger generation it creates a wonderful collaboration. With harmony between generations there will be less people on this planet who will be lonely. Reduction in loneliness is most likely going to lead to the betterment in mental and physical well-being of the members of different generation. Intergenerational togetherness can also ensure the continuation of different family traditions, and more importantly a nurturing and wholesome environment for the grandchildren and grandparents along with the sandwich generation.

But to avail these benefits there needs to be harmony between generations. This synergy is immensely important for the success and sustenance of an enterprise. Hence, let us talk about garnering IH. Garnering IH is a collaborative and participatory effort. Communication plays a unique and rather central role in it. The role of dialog is the key to achieving IH. Through multiplicity of technologies a more inclusive and participatory platform can be cultivated for different generational players. Stepping out of one's comfort zone is also going to be critical in garnering IH. Garnering IH requires a deeper understanding of behavior and psychology. It requires effective listening. It also requires challenging and defeating the inherent laziness that prevails at the physical and mental/cognitive level. Let us quickly look at the some of the theories and frameworks that may prove useful to you in garnering IH. Knowledge of these theories and frameworks is imperative as these can be put to use in different scenarios when applying the ERTH model to evaluate and monitor IH.

UNCERTAINTY REDUCTION THEORY

Uncertainty, in general and especially in social and intergenerational contexts, is stressful and sufficient to stimulate anxiety. Thoughts about being unaware about the life experiences of a person, and unable to relate to the hardships of that person can make anyone anxious before a social interaction. Unknowingly minimizing hardships of the other person creates an unnecessary schism between members of two generations. While uncertainty is beautiful and provides an opportunity to backtrack and even apologize, but for most, it is better to aim to reduce intergenerational as well as interpersonal uncertainty in social encounters. All parties involved in an interaction will be at ease and relative calm if they believe that there is relative certainty and understanding of the other person.

To help reduce some uncertainty right away, members of the Silent Generation and Baby Boomer generation may want to not expect that their grandkids always know about a given event during a certain time period. If they take on the responsibility of providing some more context and historical background instead of assuming that everyone knows about major events from half a century ago, then they can avoid being perceived as pejorative. Now, there is a slight bias at work in not knowing. Younger generations not knowing about the times, events, and hardships during certain epoch is perceived as ignorance or laziness or even apathy whereas, older generations knowing nothing about the things that matter most to the younger generation is fine or easily accepted without ascribing any negative trait to them.

On the contrary, millennials and especially Gen Z can contribute substantially to reduction in uncertainty if they can communicate their expectations with more clarity. Members of the older generation prefer clarity because it helps them navigate the request or a task at hand better. So having a direct approach using primacy might be the best strategy to reduce uncertainty. Different generations need to behave moderately differently to ensure that they are proactive in reducing uncertainty.

Asking questions is a great way to reduce uncertainty. One trick to keep in mind while asking questions is that you can disarm the person before asking a question. This can be done by prefacing the question with phrases like, "pardon my ignorance but I want to know what you meant by…?" or "If you don't mind can you give some context because I think I know what you are referring to, but I just want to be doubly sure." Before going to any intergenerational encounter which you think could be uncomfortable keep three initial questions ready. Prepare them before so that you don't become awkward in front of the person and go blank. My personal strategy to reduce uncertainty with members of other generations is to tell them they remind me of my grandparents. I circumvent conversation by conveying how I feel around them. You always feel protected and loved around your grandparents so when you tell that you are reminded of them is a way to make them feel at ease instantly.

SOCIAL PENETRATION THEORY

How does a connection or a relationship become stronger? The simple answer to this is through disclosure. Unprovoked and voluntary honest self-disclosure brings people closer. But the tricky thing here is that disclosing information about the self to another person is an individual choice where not everyone is comfortable doing it and, in the process, expressing their vulnerability, and deep emotions with the other individual. Moreover, too much too soon can also drive people away, so it is a delicate balance that one needs to achieve in the different stages of relationship building and management. How much to share and how soon to share are vital considerations. And do know that self-disclosure is often a two-way street.

Social Penetration Theory can help us understand the stage at which a relation is on the basis of the nature of self-disclosure. The typical relationship with or closeness to another person goes in a linear direction from shallow in the beginning to non-intimate and then finally to intimate levels. In intergenerational communication due to the uncertainty and the differences in the lived experiences it is very hard to strike a chord in the first meeting. Initiating self-disclosure from the trivial and shallow to the more intimate disclosures can most certainly help develop trust and empathy. Intergenerational empathy is sometimes challenging because one generation is not able to fully understand the impact of the struggles and difficulties of the other generation. Both the involved generations are not able to decide whose challenges are severe and dire. This makes the finding of the common ground difficult. Understanding the stages of relationship building and disclosure can help in finding common ground and building a rapport where having intergenerational conversations becomes less challenging and instead more gratifying and fulfilling. Incremental self-disclosure with the goal of discovering common ground and building trust in the long run is a strategy that can be informed by principles of Social Penetration Theory.

My personal strategy for self-disclosure is to share my micro-failures in different facets of life. An example of micro-failure would be losing in an intramural badminton tournament, or ruining a dish while cooking it, or some social snafu. With micro-failures you are not sharing something deeply personal that makes you uncomfortable and the other person awkward. Remember to encourage disclosure from the member of the other generation right after you finish conveying your micro-failure. "You can say something like, I burned the cake I was making for my friend's birthday. Have you ever burnt or overcooked something?"

COMMUNICATION ACCOMMODATION THEORY

Communication Accommodation Theory essentially informs us about the changes that are made in the styles of communication and behavior between two people or two groups to better attune themselves to one another. Such changes are identified as convergence. Convergence is symbolic of the adjustments that an individual or a group makes to better suit the needs and style of the other individual or group.

I can give an example from my life to help you better understand this. This example involves my honorary grandfather and my girlfriend. My honorary grandfather was born in 1930 and belonged to the silent generation, whereas my girlfriend was a millennial born in the years much closer to being in Gen Z. My honorary grandfather was hard of hearing and wore his hearing aids. Despite that he could not understand my girlfriend very well. They both were extremely fond of one another, but smooth communication was a problem. My honorary grandfather always had this issue that members of the younger Generations do not enunciate well. He also complained that members of the younger generation drop their volume as they get to the end of the sentence. So, whatever is said toward the end of the sentence, say for example the last 30% of the sentence is nothing but a whisper and lost in space. Such tendencies created issues for him earlier too but now they were exacerbated as he was hard of hearing. It is important to note that any member of any generation can have difficulties in hearing due to different disabilities, but a natural loss of hearing is much more common in the older generations then in the younger generations. I often had to nudge my girlfriend to enunciate better. I used to often suggest her to talk slowly in addition to talking loudly and retaining the same level of volume throughout the sentence. There was an adjustment that was required on her part as well as an adjustment required on my honorary grandfather's part to be more forgiving and continue to engage through checking and verifying or even summarizing what my girlfriend had said. Both had to accommodate and adjust to better understand the style of the other person. My honorary grandfather used a language which was very rich, and this often put my girlfriend in a difficult spot because she could not understand many words and many phrases that he so effortlessly used. I could not understand them either. Her English was much better than mine, but she had to adjust to being exposed to English that was rich and of a kind where every word meant something precise and was used to communicate the thought without any compromises.

The use of idioms and other time specific colloquial phrases on the one hand by the older generation and the use of modern-day slangs in informal constructions by younger generations on the other hand are both areas where different members of different generations need to work on. Members of different generations can give preference to a more streamlined and formal language in the introductory and non-intimate phases of relationship development. Once there is a higher familiarity then they can the resort back to some of their own styles. The same is also true for certain aspects of nonverbal cues such as body language, hand gestures, and facial expressions. Young people are likely to have a I don't care/lackadaisical and a slightly informal body language due to various known and unknown reasons. This type of body language is typically not preferred by members of the older generation, once again due to known and unknown reasons. There are aspects of generational insensitivity on both the sides which through the help of Communication Accommodation Theory can be identified and addressed for enhanced IH.

INTERGROUP CONTACT THEORY

When the United States was immensely divided based on racial identity, Intergroup Contact theory was introduced to study if prejudice and stigma could be reduced if more positive interactions were made possible between different racial groups. The studies conducted then suggested that a fulfilling and positive encounter with a member of other group, in this case described as contact, does play a role in slowly bringing down the stereotyping, stigmatizing, and prejudices against members of the other group.

This theory is highly relevant in the case of IH. It can be suggested that a positive contact with members of other generations through the facilitation of different art events or other programs is a welcome move. Most of the social activities are more or less age based. This allows for very little intergenerational contact and in turn further propagation and strengthening of stereotypes about other generations. For those who have never traveled to another country rely and make impressions based on what one person who traveled there told them. That person could only have encountered one bad apple but that is enough to give the entire country a bad name. Similarly, when there are very little to no intergenerational events organized then it is hard to have shared experiences. Such avenues must be created to further encourage the challenging of different stereotypes. Unless negative stereotypes are challenged, the differences will not be normalized. The focus remains on the unwantedness, or unpleasantness of a given generation instead of its awesomeness and strengths.

A few years ago, I wrote to Mattel, the company that makes Barbie to suggest to them that they should make a Grandma Barbie and a Grandpa Ken doll. Kids are used to playing with dolls that are more or less of certain ages only. Why is it that we don't have popular dolls that are representative of all generations. I was not fortunate enough, but I will surely consider it good fortune if we get to take care of our loving grandparents. Why can't we start with dolls that are in the form of grandparents. There is a famous doll of a baby, which starts crying. If you hold it right or give it fake milk bottle it will stop crying. This is how many learn to hold a baby right. Why can't we have dolls with some aging issues. Maybe we will learn to better take care of our aging parents and grandparents. Such intergroup contacts can help in improving relations by reducing biases.

During my travel in India, I came across a lady who was running a pre-school for the very poor and marginalized kids. I visited her setup, and this was because she told me that she did this one thing every month. She had collaborated with local senior centers where seniors would come to the pre-school and spend time with the kids. They would read them stories or play with them or simply share their life experiences. I found this format of inter-group contact very useful and clever.

SOCIAL EXCHANGE THEORY

Many interactions between generations are strictly instrumental or trans-actional. No generation is an island and no matter how much you try to avoid one another you will need to interact with one another in greater or lesser capacity. Since we cannot avoid interacting with one another and since a good proportion of our intergenerational communication is transactional, Social Exchange Theory can be useful to understand and apply in garnering IH.

Social Exchange Theory argues that a profit loss analysis takes place in social exchange and much of our social communication and interaction relies on the conclusion of this evaluation. In case the reward of communicating is not as much as intended then there will be a hesitation in indulging in any kind of social interaction or exchange. All generations have something unique to offer. How can the facilitators make this offering relevant and beneficial is the key here. the older generation has stories and foresight to give in addition to offering wisdom, and the younger generation has new ideas, excitement, technical expertise to offer among many other things. Promoting these as benefits, it can be made possible to encourage more frequent and stronger intergenerational dialog.

This theory is of great significance in business and government settings. Different generations have different things to offer. I can particularly recall the generational conflict within the democratic party between the leader of the party and four new members of the congress. Despite being on the same side, and belonging to a minority group, their approaches differed due to their generational belongings. They were divided based on their approaches despite having the same party affiliation. I have mentioned this incident in the

Government chapter as well. I strongly feel that we are going to see this more and more and this is where application of the Social Exchange Theory would come in handy. It is important to help members of all generations to remember that there is always something to gain from a member of another generation. This could be wisdom, technique, patience, skill, perspective, or compassion. The focus of all intergenerational interactions should be on what can one gain from any given intergenerational social exchange. This will greatly contribute positively to enhancing and garnering IH.

INTERGENERATIONAL KNOWLEDGE TRANSFER (IKT) FRAMEWORK

While important for all the five sectors, the IKT framework is especially important for established organizations. IKT framework came into existence when organizations started seeing a loss in knowledge, either due to retirement of the older generation or having a block or gap in the communication between generations. There are many aspects of institutional history and other related aspects that are all forms of tacit knowledge. These pieces are never transformed into explicit knowledge in the form of handbooks or how to guides which people can read and follow. These come through informal conversations. Most of these are remembered and retold due to them typically being unusual in the forms of narrations and stories during lunch time and other breaks.

IKT helps transform tacit knowledge into explicit knowledge. By focusing on context, content, and process one generation is able to effectively transfer knowledge from one generation to another. IKT helps hugely in smooth transition and succession through effective intergenerational knowledge transfer.

ELABORATION LIKELIHOOD MODEL

Depending on which generation you belong to, you either have a stronger preference toward more elaboration or a weaker preference for it. Typically, members of the older generation prefer more details, context, and longer explanations. This is not necessarily true of the younger generation. Members of the younger generation are more up to date with the current happenings in certain domains and having subscribed to faster pace of life do not require higher levels of explanations for context setting. This basically indicates that the requirements of each generation as well as the preferences of each generation differ from one another. Elaboration likelihood model is a very good model to understand and adapt to these differences to make communication more friendly and acceptable.

Elaboration likelihood model suggests and argues that most people process any form of information or communication through one of the two routes. Some people prefer the direct route where they focus more on the details and explanations that are provided. Such individuals' need for more information is high whereas, other group of individuals prefer low elaboration since they do not require or prefer a whole lot of details and information to act or decide. These individuals are believed to be more attuned to the peripheral route of communication messaging. Younger generation has a higher tolerance for peripheral route mainly because they can save on some time and also because this format works with their need and style of communication better.

Elaboration likelihood model is a good aid to enhance and make your intergenerational communication better as it allows us to tailor our message and the information that we want to transmit based on the needs and styles of the audience. So, this also blends in well with the learnings of Communication Accommodation Theory and they both can be used together to strengthen Intergenerational bonds.

CREATIVE AEROBICS

Ideas are the foundations of perspectives. A change in perspective can become a foundation of changes in biases. Creative Aerobics is a set of four mental exercises that allows an individual to generate ideas. Out of the four creative aerobics exercises, one of them is especially important for garnering IH. Creative Aerobics – 3, which is to find similarities between dissimilar. This exercise enables an individual to channelize his or her or their brain power to identifying similarities.

Something to note here is that human beings are trained and attuned to identify differences. We can instantly identify all the differences without putting in much effort. But that is not the case when it comes to similarities. We are not trained to identify similarities. This does not mean that we don't have the ability, we simply don't exercise it. And if you think about it much of the challenges in the world are due to differences. Difference in opinion, approach, ideology, religion, practice, nationality, race, gender, and more. And we humans continue to focus on these because they come to us naturally. It is easy to talk about the difference between the generations but it is very hard to apply oneself to identifying similarities between generations. Through Creative Aerobics three we learn to exercise this ability. Once we are able to see more similarities, which already exist, then our attitude and approach also changes. When we realize that members of other generations are much more like us and that too in so many ways then it is easy to collaborate.

So, before any intergenerational gathering, ask everyone to spend the first five minutes thinking about 10 similarities between them and members of a different generation. This identification will create a different mindset and will contribute greatly to garnering IH.

CONCLUSION

Garnering IH should be attempted with a singular focus. To leverage the strategic power of our enterprises, harmony between generations is paramount. Despite recognizing it, harmony is taken for granted. But harmony is not something that we let exist. We, humans are the masters of disruption and chaos. This means that to achieve and sustain IH, we have to work for it. The natural order of IH is not going to restore itself unchecked. And that is why garnering IH is the need of the hour.

The theories that I have supplied above are just the starting point. They are pretty much like sharing a recipe. Once the recipe is shared, one has to execute it. Proper ingredients need to be purchased, and then the cooking process needs to be initiated and then finally tasting needs to be done to see if the food suited your palate or not and if there is anything more or different needed.

These theories are educated guesses tested over time to increase our confidence in an outcome. These theories have been tested in many studies and contexts and have been included here because they have a possibility of working similarly in this context as well. The first step is to make people aware of these theories. Prepare small chits and place them in front of everyone before the start of a meeting or a class or dinner or religious service. This will remind them to be more respectful or trusting.

The one thing that is critical is honesty. There is no substitute for honesty. Through honesty, it becomes relatively easy to foster respect and trust. Honesty can also aid in generating empathy as it gives an accurate idea to the other person about what you are going through and what are the challenges at your end. Encouraging people to be honest will go a long way in garnering IH.

9

INTERGENERATIONAL HARMONY IS THE FUTURE

If we learn from the mistakes of the past, then we can improve our future. A solid way to improve our future is through IH. IH is important because it is a strong predictor of the survival and success of an enterprise. Intergenerational Harmony is a prerequisite for enterprises to thrive in the present and in the time to come. Intergenerational Harmony is a state of existence. It is a state of being with countless potentialities. Any enterprise with high IH is more likely survive and succeed in comparison with an enterprise with low IH. If the human enterprise wants to increase its chances of success and survival, then it has to enhance its IH in all the sectors of human life and endeavors. And for those who cannot work toward enhancing IH in all sectors of human life and endeavor, this book highlights five mega-sectors where IH is critical. Family, Government, Religion, Corporation, and Education are the five mission critical sectors where the presence of high levels of IH is a must. This is because these sectors have a broad impact on many key facets of human civilization.

I have elaborated each of the five sectors in previous chapters in this book. I have highlighted the major areas of conflict and differences. This should provide the reader a unique insight into the root causes of the differences. This awareness will enable my reader to respond differently to an intergenerational stimulus in different settings. If a multigenerational family can enjoy one meal together in joy and delight, then the purpose of this book is served. If one legislation is passed with the combined might and support of all generations then the purpose of this book is served. If a daughter continues to work in her family business and does not quit due to intergenerational conflict, then the purpose of this book is served. The main purpose of this book is to instigate a state of existence and being that can help in giving our mother earth a chance to nourish us for longer.

INSTANCES OF IH

The crisis of multigenerationality can manifest itself in many ways. I will share with you two real-life examples and instances of unique ways in which generational harmony was embraced and an attempt was made to enhance it.

NATIONAL CREATORS AWARD

In the month of March of 2024, on the auspicious day of Maha Shivratri (a Hindu Festival), which was also serendipitously the International Women's Day, the Prime Minister of the Republic of India awarded and felicitated dozens of social media content creators as part of his superb new initiative called the National Creators Award.[1] This was the first of its kind government sponsored and organized award function with intergenerational harmony as its essence. In his speech, the Honorable PM of India said that it is our duty to recognize what engages and excites the younger generation and celebrate it. We, in India, have identified your important role of spreading awareness, about important topics as well as positioning India and projecting India's Soft Power globally through your creations. We want to thank you and celebrate you. We also want to do a collab with you. He also offered some pointers and suggestions for the type of content and some areas in which more work can be done. He publicly appreciated the younger generation and offered them a platform while extending a hand to come together to bring in further inter-generational harmony.

This was one of the best moves to include younger generation in the work of nation building through their interests, abilities, and skills. He even mentioned in his speech that it is important to keep in touch with times and you guys are in touch with the times, so it becomes our responsibility to connect and engage with you. This event is available on YouTube, and you should watch it. You will see so many of the theories mentioned in the earlier chapter in action. This is by far one of the best attempts by any government globally thus far to close the gap between generations. I am absolutely certain that this will further strengthen IH in the Indian subcontinent and ready it for the future.

NATIONAL SORRY DAY IN AUSTRALIA

Australian parliament had decreed a practice of separating children from their families. These children belonged the Aboriginal and Torres Strait Islander descent. This terrible practice that was initiated with the said noble goal of giving the aboriginals an opportunity to enhance the lives of aboriginal children continued in Australia for 60 years causing immense grief and trauma to hundreds of thousands of families. Generational trauma lingers around for a very long time. The children that were separated are known as the Stolen Generation in Australia. Research also suggested later on that there were many unintended consequences on the life and overall social balance. This act severely disturbed the IH in the country of Australia.

Recognizing the grave wrong done in the past, and in an effort to take the first step in the direction of enhancing harmony among the people and especially the ones affected by the Stolen Generation, the Australian Government declared May 26 the National Sorry Day or the National Day of Healing. The Australian Prime Minister in 2008 issued a public apology for the wrong doings of the past and extended a hand of friendship and support to many. This one act has encouraged many other instances of respecting the autonomy of others. Apologizing and following up on the rectified course goes to create trust between generations. Generational trauma is hard to heal but it can be prevented from exacerbating.

LET'S ADOPT ERTH

In addition to the above two examples of attempts made at encouraging IH, there are also examples of young generations coming together against pollution and further destruction of Earth. To save earth I have offered you ERTH. Stereotypes pertaining to other generations will need to systematically be identified, challenged and eliminated by executing interventions with the help of ERTH. ERTH, by now, you would know stands for empathy, respect, trust, and honesty.

ERTH is the practical tool that can help you measure the presence and absence of IH in your family or your corporation or the people of a nation. IH is a condition where different generational stakeholders within an enterprise are working in synergy to elevate and capitalize on the strengths of one another. According to the ERTH model, Intergenerational Harmony is made up of four dimensions. These four dimensions are Empathy, Respect, Trust, and Honesty. Together they form make up Intergenerational Harmony. By working on Empathy, Respect, Trust, and Honesty, we can succeed in increasing IH. In its optimal form, IH is the best antidote we have against the onslaught of crisis of Multigenerationality.

I have also offered the Dimensional Cross and the 5-star rating system that is simple and easy to deploy. The 5-star system gives a quick insight into the level of IH within the given population. If there is a need to work on increasing IH then you can consult the Dimensional cross. The Dimensional Cross will provide a deeper and nuanced understanding of all the four elements of ERTH. This detailed analysis is very visual in nature for quick interpretation. The goal is to see less and less of red and more and more of other colors. Based on the color scheme of the Dimensional Cross, it becomes easy to identify the dimension which requires maximum work. All the four have to be balanced. If one is less and others are more or vice versa then IH is only a goal and not something that you can achieve. If you work on the intel from the Dimensional Cross, using the different theories and tips given all throughout the chapter then your rating in the 5-star rating system will increase. If you have, 2-stars, you should increase to 3 and then 4 and then 5.

It is important to note here that there are different ways to understand and look at a generation. I have supplied ample examples of the alternate under-standings of generations. ERTH is universal. What I mean by that is that regardless of the type and nature of a generation, ERTH can still be deployed. It does not work for only one type of understanding of generation. It can be applied to measure the presence or absence of IH in all sorts of generational understanding. The biggest advantage of IH is that it can be measured and evaluated. Systematic activities and programs can be launched to work on either all or some aspects of ERTH.

CONCLUSION

IH is the future. Without it there is only conflict and no real future. Leaders belonging to all the five sectors have to pay attention to enhance IH in their sector. Family is the logical starting point. If Government buys in, then its reach can extend to Education. If you as a leader or owner of a Business want to increase your profit you will need to be on the right side of IH. Religion, or I should say, some religions don't have much of a future without IH. They will bleed out. No amount of money or resources will be able to prevent your ceasing to exist. The wise will heed to ERTH because the crisis is only going to become worse. While there is much talk about the future, there is one looming variable that we don't know about as much as we know about the other generations.

What about Generation Alpha?

Generation Alpha is growing and growing up fast. We don't have much of a clue at the moment what will its impact be on the storm. It is bound to stir the hornets' nest, which is already not at peace. What will be the dynamic of Gen Alpha with Gen X or with the Millennials.

I will leave you with two more analogies as food for thought for you.

What is the relation between roots, trunk, branches, leaves, fruits, and flowers. To me they are all different expressions of generations of growth and prosperity of a tree. The Silent generation, Baby Boomers, Gen X, Millennials, Gen Z, and Gen Alpha are the same. What happens to a tree where all its elements are not working in synergy?

Finally, imagine that you have to go to a party. You get dressed up really well. Just as you are about to enter the party you realize that there is a pebble in your shoe. Despite being dressed so well and being amidst amazing company, where will your attention be?

Absence of Intergenerational Harmony is like a pebble in the shoe. Unwanted, annoying, and thankfully fixable. So, lets come together to harness the power of Intergenerational Harmony.

NOTE

1.   https://innovateindia.mygov.in/national-creators-award-2024/;   https://y20india.in/national-creators-award-2024/

Printed and bound by CPI Group (UK) Ltd, Croydon, CR0 4YY

14/11/2024

14593074-0005